THE WALLACE NOTESTEIN ESSAYS, NO. 3

YALE HISTORICAL PUBLICATIONS

DAVID HORNE, EDITOR

*Published under the direction of the
Department of History with assistance from the income
of the Frederick John Kingsbury Memorial Fund*

C U S H I N G S T R O U T

The Pragmatic Revolt in American History:

Carl Becker and Charles Beard

New Haven

Y A L E U N I V E R S I T Y P R E S S

© *1958 by Yale University Press, Inc.*

*Set in Monotype Aldine Bembo type and
printed in the United States of America by
the Printing-Office of the Yale University Press
New Haven, Connecticut and reprinted by The
Murray Printing Company, Forge Village, Massachusetts.*

First published, October, 1958

Second printing, August, 1959
Library of Congress catalog card number: 58–11262.

Dedicated with Gratitude and Affection
to
My Mother and Father

Acknowledgments

NOTHING is more likely to shake the historian's confidence in his power to tell the truth than making the effort to give a just account of his intellectual debts. If I have failed to include them all, it is not from any lack of a sense of gratitude. For arousing and shaping my interest in the philosophy of history I owe more than I can ever adequately reckon to the immensely provocative teaching of John W. Miller at Williams College. Since my undergraduate years I have been influenced, as philosophers will recognize, by the writings of R. G. Collingwood, Benedetto Croce, Michael Oakeshott, Raymond Aron, and Ortega y Gasset. Most of the research and thinking which went into the making of this essay were done at Harvard University in 1951–52, for a thesis in American Civilization. I was fortunate in having Perry Miller and also Oscar Handlin for advisers; they gave me, besides the high example of their own work, the needed encouragement and freedom to work out my salvation on a topic which less imaginative and more paternalistic mentors might have rejected. I hope the former will feel that his efforts to keep me from ever forgetting the humanity of my two subjects were not wasted.

This extensively revised and condensed version of my thesis owes much to my colleagues at Yale. David M. Potter has been especially generous with his time, criticism, and support, greatly aiding me in clarifying and organizing my argument. George W. Pierson has very skillfully pruned many a literary thicket of my own making, and Harry Rudin's benignly critical eye particularly helped me in my efforts to deal fairly with the controversy over Beard's foreign policy.

I especially want to mention the value of many discussions of Becker with Bernard Bailyn of Harvard, who also was very generous with bibliographical suggestions when we were graduate students. Another friend, Howard H. Quint of the University of South Carolina, put me on the track of some articles by Beard I would otherwise have missed. Several distinguished and busy people have done me the honor and service of answering requests for information, letters, or interviews. I shall long remember my correspondence and meeting with Mary R. Beard as one of the most delightful rewards of my work. Mr. Justice Felix Frankfurter and Brigadier General Charles A. Lindbergh have been extremely courteous in responding to my inquiries. A former colleague and friend of Beard's, Harry Elmer Barnes, has shown me much kindness—all the more appreciated because of our vigorous differences of opinion —by making letters from his file available to me. I have also benefited from courtesies extended to me by Beard's son-in-law, Alfred Vagts. William Beard and Mrs. Vagts have granted me permission to quote from certain letters of their father's which are now part of the Villard Papers in the Houghton Library at Harvard University, the private file of Barnes, or the Becker Papers in the Mann Library at Cornell University. To the libraries of these institutions I am grateful also for permission to use their materials on my subject. Richard A. Newhall, a former teacher of mine at Williams College, and W. Stull Holt of the University of Washington have graciously allowed me the use of certain letters from their correspondence with Becker.

It is conventional to absolve all those who have helped from any responsibility for the writer's judgments or errors, but in this case the reminder is genuinely needful. My topic and its treatment are inevitably controversial and everyone who has assisted me would probably want to dissent at numerous points from my argument. It is also a ritual to conclude with thanks to one's wife, but mine deserves uncommon credit not just for maintaining my morale, which sometimes badly needed propping, but also for casting a cool eye any editor would envy over every page of the many versions of this manuscript. Finally, I am indebted to the Yale Fund for Young Scholars, which materially assisted in the publication of this book.

CUSHING STROUT

New Haven, Conn.
January 1958.

Contents

NARROW and dogmatic thinkers and commentators often have an immense vogue and many followers; but those who grasp at the hem of greater things are more likely to command an enduring influence on thought and practice . . . Their shortcomings may be painfully evident, but the amplitude of their reach commands long-time respect—a tribute to their powers.—*Charles A. Beard*

IF SUCH a criticism should take us even into the domain of the philosophy of history, let us not be dismayed; for it is possible that in seeking to avoid having a philosophy of history the historian does not succeed in not having one; perhaps after all he succeeds only in having a bad one.—*Carl L. Becker*

Introduction

EVER since the 19th century one of the most striking characteristics of the modern mind has been its preoccupation with history. In earlier times the historical sense was neither sophisticated nor pervasive, but now even science and religion, long-revered guardians of timeless truths, are approached historically. "To regard all things in their historical setting appears, indeed," as Carl Becker has said, "to be an instructual procedure of the modern mind. We do it without thinking, because we can scarcely think at all without doing it."[1] This relatively new intellectual awareness of the historical dimension of life has been paralleled by the modern tendency toward secularization, the acceptance of the concrete world of human history as the source of ultimate values and fulfillment. The modern mind has looked to history not only as a mode of understanding but also as a final destiny. It has been primarily concerned with the secular problems posed by the workings of the historical process, and it has had the confidence to believe that those problems could be solved in and through the very process which generated them.

Liberalism, among modern historical forces, has characteristically expressed this secular commitment to control of the historical process, though, paradoxically, its confidence has been based less on the development of historical thought than on the new powers which natural science and technology have produced. Because man has learned to control nature, liberals have believed that men could achieve progress in history.

1. *The Heavenly City of the Eighteenth-century Philosophers* (New Haven, Yale University Press, 1932), pp. 18–19.

This modern faith in history as both an intellectual inquiry and a progressive process is now suffering a profound crisis. "On its intellectual side, the crisis of our time," a contemporary philosopher of liberalism has claimed, "is a crisis in our interpretation of history; in particular, it is a crisis in the attitude we ought to take toward the liberal interpretation of modern history."[2] This critical situation has been produced, ironically, by the development of the historical spirit itself. The extension of the historical approach has created, in Karl Mannheim's phrase, an "intellectual twilight which dominates our epoch and in which all values and points of view appear in their genuine relativity."[3] In this strange light the authority of historical inquiry and of liberalism itself has been called into question, for a thoroughgoing relativism must shake all standards by destroying their claim to absoluteness. When all points of view are understood as passing phases of a historical process, neither the historian as knower nor the liberal as philosopher can claim a place to stand outside the stream of history. In this twilight it will appear pretentious to make the affirmation that history can be either understood or controlled. Yet if it cannot make this assertion, the modern mind, so committed to the centrality of history, will have confessed bankruptcy.

Carl L. Becker and Charles A. Beard have an important place in American thought because of their closeness to this crisis of the modern mind. These profound dilemmas were theirs. They helped produce them; they tried to solve them. Above all, they suffered the consequences of recognizing them: the inability to work with the serene complacency that there were no fundamental problems that had not already been solved and the incurring of the puzzled hostility of those scholars for whom conventional assumptions and habits were still adequate. Some of their critics have even implied

2. Charles Frankel, *The Case for Modern Man* (New York, Harper and Bros., 1955), p. 5.
3. *Ideology and Utopia: An Introduction to the Sociology of Knowledge*, trans. Louis Wirth and Edward Shils (New York, Harcourt Brace, 1949), p. 76.

that Becker and Beard, in their radical skepticism about traditional assumptions, betrayed their craft and its standards. Loosely drawn analogies have been made between their views and those of thinkers who allegedly prepared the way for the rise of fascism in Europe. It has even been charged that the powerful influence of Becker and Beard on American thought has served to justify an American brand of totalitarianism disguised as liberalism.[4] Such critics, for all their lip service to history, are surprisingly unhistorical, for they make no attempt to discover how and why Becker and Beard acquired their problems, as if the significance of new ideas could be determined apart from a knowledge of the point to which previous inquiry had brought the problem. To some historians, also, the lesson of Becker and Beard may seem to be that in turning to philosophy the historian can only jeopardize his tradition and faith, but, as Ortega y Gasset has said, "in truth it is not that philosophy killed tradition and faith, but that tradition and faith sickened and died, and philosophy had to take up the mantle as best she could."[5]

Becker and Beard tried to ground the study of history in a new philosophy, appropriate to the development of modern thought. Both men played the role of skeptical gadflies to the orthodoxies of their profession. They did not rest content with the conventional "contribution to knowledge" made by historical monographs on narrowly limited subjects. As Becker noted, "the trouble with so many contributions to knowledge is that they are made by scholars who know all the right answers but none of the right questions."[6]

---

4. See, for example, Chester McArthur Destler, "Some Observations on Contemporary Historical Theory," *American Historical Review* [AHR], 55 (1950), 525; James C. Malin, *On the Nature of History: Essays about History and Dissidence* (Ann Arbor, Michigan, 1954), pp. 275–84.

5. José Ortega y Gasset, *Concord and Liberty,* trans. Helene Weyl (New York, W. W. Norton, 1946), p. 114.

6. Review of Henry O. Taylor, *A Historian's Creed;* Gaetano Salvemini, *Historian and Scientist;* and Sir Charles Oman, *On the Writing of History,* in *AHR,* 45 (1940), 593.

Beard's scorn for the routine procedure of much academic historiography was equally sharp. The "pontificalia" of the guild seemed to demand, he felt, that the historian should never "apply to the reputable lore of the middling orders the Socratic elenchus," nor "essay the role of Jeremiah against the Philistines or invoke the spirit of Buckle or Darwin."[7] Becker's weapons were a subtle wit and a skeptical irony, while Beard was armed with a fearless passion for controversy and a sardonic contempt for the pieties of "respectable" opinion. They had quite different temperaments. Becker was content with the professor's life, quite satisfied that teachers should be "confined for life in this delightful country of the mind, with nothing 'to do,' privileged to go on as best they could with the great adventure."[8] Beard's sense of adventure was more active. He left Columbia University in 1917, resigning in protest against restrictions on academic freedom, with no regrets for leaving behind a world where he had found "too much calm, not enough passion; above all too many sacred traditions that must be conserved . . . too many books, not enough strife of experience; too many students, not enough seekers."[9] As a leading spirit in the New York Bureau for Municipal Research, as a consultant on municipal problems in both Japan and Yugoslavia, and as a dairy farmer in New Milford, Connecticut, where he tried to organize the local farmers, he found new outlets for his enormous energy. For Becker—constitutionally

7. "History and History," *Nation, 111* (1920), 417.

8. "On Being a Professor," *Unpopular Review, 7* (1917), 345. The best account of Becker's life and character is in Charlotte Watkins Smith, *Carl Becker: On History and the Climate of Opinion* (Ithaca, Cornell University Press, 1956), pp. 1–42.

9. "Political Science," in *Research in the Social Sciences: Its Fundamental Methods and Objectives,* ed. Wilson Gee (New York, Macmillan, 1929), pp. 289–90. For personal accounts of Beard see Arthur W. Macmahon, "Charles Austin Beard as a Teacher," *Political Science Quarterly, 65* (1950), 1–19; Matthew Josephson, "Charles A. Beard: A Memoir," *Virginia Quarterly Review, 25* (1949), 585–602; Mary R. Beard, *The Making of Charles A. Beard* (New York, Exposition Press, 1955), 9–36.

shy, plagued with stomach ulcers much of his life, and convinced with Pascal that "Thought makes the whole dignity of man; therefore endeavor to think well, that is the only morality"—the detachment of the academic world from the pressures of action was its chief charm. Even as a teacher he had little desire to mold the minds of undergraduates by either showmanship or discipline and ran his classes as informally as possible both at the University of Kansas, where he taught for fourteen years, and at Cornell University, where he joined the faculty just as Beard was resigning from academic life, in 1917. Whereas Beard had been a dramatic and popular lecturer and a prodigiously productive writer with a wide public influence, Becker's aloofness made him seem a listless teacher to the ordinary student and his painstaking devotion to history as a literary art reduced his output to more modest proportions, though its special stamp of wit and polish gave him an equally appreciative, if smaller, audience.

For all their personal differences Becker and Beard could join forces in their battles with the dogmas of the day. Inheritors of a tradition in which theological or scientific ambitions controlled the prevailing philosophy of history, they tried to establish the independence of historical thought. In revolt against the concentration of an earlier generation of historians upon the institutional history of legal and political forms, they were part of the modern movement for the study of social, economic, and intellectual history. When the dust had settled, Clio's image had been radically transformed. From her position as a grave, impartial goddess, above the battle, she had been thrust into the thick of the struggle as a humble warrior by the new pragmatic relativism which Becker and Beard had developed. From her pedestal where she had, in a dry, antiquarian tone, addressed her pupils on constitutions, laws, and political events, she was sent down into the market place to take notes in the new antiformalist spirit on the social, economic, and cultural conflicts that agitated the populace. Working in these relatively new directions, Becker and Beard helped shape the whole tenor of contemporary historical writing. As liberals, who had come to maturity during the reform era of progressivism and faced the crises of two world wars and the rise of modern totalitarianism, they had another basis for alliance. Heirs of the confidence of the Enlightenment in the secularization of society, the spread of liberty and self-government, and the promise of progress through science and technology, they sought to harmonize their hopes for America with their philosophical and historical thinking.

Like most intellectuals, challenged by the terrible events of modern history, their thought did not pass unscathed through its ordeal by fire. The scars now need close attention by those not only anxious to heal the wounds but also willing to risk drastic surgery. Carl Becker and Charles Beard had at least the necessary courage to face the problems of that "intellectual twilight" in which all values and points of view appear in their historical relativity. "At this point in history," as Karl Mannheim has said, "when all things which concern man and the structure and elements of history itself are suddenly revealed to us in a new light, it behooves us in our scientific thinking to become masters of the situation, for it is not inconceivable that sooner than we suspect, as has often been the case before in history, this vision may disappear, the opportunity may be lost, and the world will once again present a static, uniform, and inflexible countenance."[10]

The implications of the revolt against scientifically oriented historical positivism, led by Becker and Beard, can be fully understood only by an interpretation which seeks to comprehend the organic relationship of their philosophies of history, their historical writings, and their political outlooks. Such unity as exists will not, of course, have the neatness and clarity of an abstract philosophical system, because both men were basically historians, primarily concerned with the untidy affairs of men, past and present, rather than with the symmetry of axioms and absolutes. Yet they were highly re-

10. *Ideology and Utopia*, p. 76.

flective and self-conscious historians, eager to philosophize, whose
work has at least the living logic of a point of view struggling for
expression and development. Though I have in the following pages
given separate attention to each of the three main phases of their
thought, I have tried to see them in relationship to each other.

Becker and Beard had strong individual characteristics as persons,
as historians, and as philosophers. In treating them together within
the covers of a single book I have had no intention of blurring those
differences. For this reason I have analyzed their peculiar contribution to my theme in separate chapters after Chapter One, which ex-
pounds their common tradition and setting. Despite their differences, however, I believe they can be fruitfully studied together as
innovators who share important common assumptions in philosophy, history, and politics.

I realize that philosophical issues about history's purpose, method,
and value seem alien to many historians. These are questions they
would happily leave to the philosophers, who do not have the
pleasure and the duty of dealing with the detailed and documentary
world of the working historian. Many philosophers, for their part,
are likely to alternate between condemnation of the historian for
his philosophical indifference and disdain for his logic when he
overcomes it. They are confident that the philosophy of history is
something for them to establish. These attitudes are quite under-
standable. Yet there are some historians and some philosophers who
realize that such a tidy division of labor cannot realistically be maintained. They know that American philosophers have tended to
neglect the philosophy of history, because of their absorption in
theology, science, logic, or language, and that historians cannot
without self-deception forever ignore the philosophical problems
in which their daily practice is implicated. It is to these scholars,
who, as philosophers, feel that historians have something to tell
them and, as historians, feel that philosophers can help them, that
my book is especially addressed. Inevitably I have been forced to be
both historian and philosopher. It is a risky venture to engage in

two dangerous trades. As a historian my heart belongs to the concrete world of history; as a critic of my own discipline my head has
obligations, contracted by my problems and questions, to the abstract world of philosophy. I have tried to make the best of this
difficult situation, taking comfort in the brave example of Carl
Becker and Charles Beard. In criticizing them I plead guilty not to
arrogance but to admiring emulation of their own willingness to
engage in controversy.

My strategy has been to examine in Part I the tradition of American historical thought in which they found themselves and also their
own theoretical contribution to it. Part II is a scrutiny of their
general reflections and specific researches on the historical process
itself. The concluding section, Part III, is an investigation of their
troubled relationship to the practical historical conflicts of their own
time. My argument and exposition require the frequent use of
several concepts which may, at first glance, seem as puzzling as
they are irritating to admirers of Anglo-Saxon simplicity of style.
I do not believe it is possible to give absolutely intelligible definitions
apart from some specific context of discussion, but as mere signposts
the following explanation of my principal terms may be useful:

Scientific history or *historical positivism*. The attempt to understand
history as both a discipline and a process in terms drawn from the
natural sciences. There are two kinds of *scientific historians:* those who
seek to establish some all-embracing theory of the structure and direction of the course of historical events, which are assumed to fall
into a pattern with the regularity and predictability of phenomena
in the natural sciences, and those who find the substance of history
in isolated, externalized happenings, which are the "facts" it is the
historian's sole duty to establish in a spirit of neutral, passive, detachment.

Determinism. The belief that all events are subject to a universal
pattern of lawfulness which can be explained causally without
reference to any human factors of will and thought which are not
themselves the inevitable consequences of certain causal antecedents.

A particular form of this belief is *economic determinism* which holds that changes in the structure of society are due in the last analysis to economic causes arising out of modes of production.

Pragmatic or *skeptical relativism*. The skeptical factor in the theory is the assertion that the historian's account of the past can be genuine knowledge only to a very limited degree and is fundamentally a temporary appraisal, based on the historian's interests and values, which are themselves conditioned by his particular time, circumstances, and personality. The pragmatic factor in the theory is the assumption that historical reconstructions are functional adjustments of an organism to its environment, made to satisfy the current needs and hopes of the historian's social group. The emphasis tends to fall on the central role of plans and hopes for future betterment as determinants of the historian's act of historical synthesis.

Antiformalism. I have borrowed this phrase from Morton G. White. It stands here primarily for a concern with the vital matrix of social and economic forces and conditions which underlie institutional forms and theoretical constructions. As a temper of mind, *antiformalism* tends to make an invidious contrast between the dynamic and the static, history and logic, experience and principle, practical adjustment and formal order, the utilitarian and the elegant. For the *antiformalist* the first term of each antithesis is the honorific one.

Technocratic rationalism. The assumption that society can and should be understood, organized, and controlled by techniques which are derived from the natural sciences and engineering, in order to establish a "rational" way of life.

Liberalism. Its adherents put their political trust in limited government, democratically organized, and in the value of maintaining the civil liberties of the individual in matters of speech, press, belief, and assembly. Philosophically the liberal puts his confidence in secular, critical thought rather than in theological dogma or faith in the sanctity of any leader, group, institution, or creed; and he finds his ultimate values not in any transcendental realm, but in the region of finite, secular life itself. To this camp I freely acknowledge my own commitment, while reserving my right to criticize the corrupting or confusion of liberalism by an indulgence on the part of some liberals of utopian views about reason, social planning, or historical progress.

PART ONE

The Revolt of Relativism

CHAPTER ONE

Background to Revolution

CARL BECKER AND CHARLES BEARD started a controversy over the purpose of historical writing and the limits of the historian's objectivity that still agitates American historians and philosophers. Some of their most vigorous critics have even charged that the views of Becker and Beard have thoroughly dominated contemporary American historians and historical theorists. Allowing for the tendency of alarmists to exaggerate the power of whatever they brand menacing, one can see, at least in the present, a striving for a new sophistication about history, provoked by the questions insistently raised by Becker and Beard. In 1946 the Committee on Theory and Practice in Historical Study, set up by the Social Science Research Council under the chairmanship of Merle Curti, produced a report which reflected the heuristic influence of Becker and Beard.[1] Their role has been to challenge custom and promote inquiry, rather than to provide an adequate philosophy upon which the historical profession could agree. It is the function of pioneers to blaze a trail, not to establish a settlement. New ideas, like other historical forces, have no immaculate conception. In the struggle for life they emerge entangled in the present, encrusted with the past, and striving dimly for the future.

Becker and Beard worked under peculiarly American disadvantages. In Europe there has been a modern tradition of philosopher-

1. "Theory and Practice in Historical Study," Report of the Committee on Historiography, Social Science Research Council, *Bulletin 54* (1946). Beard wrote pp. 3–14, 105–8.

historians, like Wilhelm Dilthey, Benedetto Croce, Ortega y Gasset, Raymond Aron, and R. G. Collingwood. But only very recently in America have philosophers, long dominated by religious or scientific interests, begun to center their attention on the problems of the philosophy of history. Even pragmatism—which stimulated both Becker and Beard because of its concern for the temporal, the changing, and the finite as opposed to the traditional search for the timeless, the static, and the infinite—grew out of the scientific controversy over evolution. History was not a major theme of the philosophers of pragmatism. It was peripheral to James' interest in psychology and religion, Dewey's in education and science, Peirce's in metaphysics and cosmology. For ideas about history Becker and Beard were compelled to look to Europe, to their fellow historians, or to themselves. It was natural, then, that they found their point of departure in the controversies among American historians over the philosophy of history, getting what help they could from their reading of European philosophers who, unfortunately for Becker's and Beard's understanding of them, belonged to an alien tradition.

Historical writing in America had been in the hands of amateurs until the emergence of the professional guild of historians in the late 19th century. By the turn of the 20th century historical seminars, on the German model, had been established in the great universities for two decades; American historians had formed a national association (1884) and published a scholarly review for the regular dissemination of their findings (1895); sober, multivolumed works and meticulously researched monographs, written by academically trained historians, had become the reigning style. The study of history had come of age in America, and it entered upon its majority with the determination to be "scientific." This emergence of a new professional discipline was coincident with the impact of the idea of evolution on American thought. The first president of the newly formed American Historical Association, Andrew D. White, spoke for his generation when he confessed that what had stimulated him most as a historian had been "the atmosphere coming from the great thought of Darwin and Spencer—an atmosphere in which history became less and less a matter of annals, and more and more a record of the unfolding of humanity."[2] The language of his presidential address to his colleagues, with its references to "cycles of birth, growth, and decay," to "laws of development," and to the "evolution of that which is best in man and in society,"[3] reflected the new scientific aspirations of historians.

The positivism of Auguste Comte had, before Darwin's impact, held out the promise of a scientific history. John W. Draper, an American scientist, inventor, and historian, had even analyzed the past in terms of periodic stages, reminiscent of Comte's philosophy of history, and had argued that just as the astronomer prophesies future events deduced from his knowledge of the laws under which the celestial bodies move, "so may the Historian, who relies on the immutability of Nature, predict the inevitable course through which a nation must pass."[4] In the next generation a much greater historian, Henry Adams, was also profoundly influenced by Comte. In 1884, while working on his famous *History of the United States,* Adams wrote Francis Parkman, welcoming the application of scientific determinism to history:

> The more I write, the more confident I feel that before long a new school of history will rise which will leave us antiquated. Democracy is the only subject for history. I am satisfied that the purely mechanical development of the human mind in society must appear in a great democracy so clearly, for want of disturbing elements, that in another generation psychology,

2. *Autobiography of Andrew Dickson White* (London, Macmillan, 1905), 1, 42.

3. "On Studies in General History and the History of Civilization," American Historical Association, *Papers,* 1 (1886), 51.

4. Quoted by Donald E. Emerson, "Hildrith, Draper, and Scientific History," in *Historiography and Urbanization: Essays in American History in Honor of W. Stull Holt,* ed. Eric F. Goldman (Baltimore, Johns Hopkins University Press, 1941), p. 155.

physiology, and history will join in proving man to have as fixed and necessary development as that of a tree; and almost as unconscious.[5]

Adams himself, in collaboration with his brother Brooks, was devoted to a lifelong search for a science of history as a process of mental evolution controlled by a general formula. "One sought only a spool," he said, "on which to wind the thread of history without breaking it."[6] Combining Newton's law of inverse squares, Maxwell's theory of gases, Kelvin's law of entropy, and Gibbs' law of phase, he built his final theory on what he took to be the scientific evidence for the degradation of energy in a universe that was running down. Working on the basis of these analogies, congenial to his acid pessimism and sense of frustration as well as to his ironic sense of humor, he periodized history into various phases of the current of thought which was supposedly accelerating toward the fatal year 1921, when the human mind was to reach the limit of its possibilities. For all its dilettante science and alarmist conclusions Adams' speculation was an ambitious attempt to realize the ideal of scientific history shared by his generation.

Most historians of the day found their scientific inspiration not in Comte but in Darwin or Spencer. No serious student or imaginative teacher of history, wrote Henry Adams, could in that day have helped feeling that "he stood on the brink of a great generalization that would reduce all history under a law" or keep from dreaming of "the immortality that would be achieved by the man who should successfully apply Darwin's method to the facts of human history."[7]

5. Letter to Parkman, Dec. 21, 1884, in *Henry Adams and His Friends: A Collection of His Unpublished Letters,* comp. Harold Dean Cater (Boston, Houghton Mifflin, 1947), p. 134.

6. *The Education of Henry Adams* (New York, Modern Library, 1931), p. 472. The best interpretation of Adams as historian is William Jordy, *Henry Adams: Scientific Historian,* New Haven, Yale University Press, 1952.

7. *The Degradation of the Democratic Dogma,* intro. Brooks Adams (New York, Macmillan, 1919), p. 127.

Darwin himself had suggested that the progress of the United States was a result of "natural selection" and the Anglo-Saxon emigration to the West the climactic, organizing event of all history.[8] For American historians Darwin seemed to have provided a scientific basis for their confidence in the superiority of Anglo-Saxon political institutions and to have pointed the way toward a conception of the historical process as a slow genetic development of progress from the ancient seeds of contemporary institutions to their present flowering. It was in this atmosphere that John Fiske and Herbert Baxter Adams formulated their popular theories of the origin of New England towns in Teutonic village communities in an effort to trace the lineage of democracy back to Saxon roots. It was this "germ theory of politics," as it came to be called, that Adams, an important figure in the founding of historical seminars and the new professional guild of historians, taught at Johns Hopkins University, the mecca for young historians of the day. There they learned from him that there was "a subtle genealogy" in human institutions, just as there was with every individual, who held within himself "a long train of lives, carrying the hereditary forces of family and race —a ghostly train of progenitors."[9] The doctoral dissertation of Frederick Jackson Turner, "The Character and Influence of the Indian Trade in Wisconsin: A Study of the Trading Post as an Institution," made its bow to Adams by tracing the institution back to the Phoenicians. A few years later, in an address to the American Historical Association in 1893, Turner, in conscious revolt against "the germ theory" of his teacher, delivered his famous paper "The Significance of the Frontier in American History." Yet Turner himself, whose work was a powerful force in shaping the character of modern American historical writing, appealed to the idea of evolution in making his case for the derivation of American democracy

8. *The Descent of Man* (New York, Appleton, 1871), *1*, 172–3.
9. Quoted by Richard T. Ely, "A Sketch of the Life and Services of Herbert Baxter Adams," in *Herbert Baxter Adams: Tributes of Friends* (Baltimore, Johns Hopkins University Press, 1902), p. 41.

and national character from the ever-moving frontier. "The history of our political institutions, our democracy," he wrote, with an implied rebuke of "the germ theory," "is not a history of imitation, of simple borrowing; it is a history of the evolution and adaptation of organs in response to changed environment, a history of the origin of new political species." American democracy, he asserted, "came from no theorist's dreams of the German forest. It came, stark and strong and full of life, from the American forest."[10] This geographical determinism challenged Adams' search for the "ghostly train of progenitors," but both men were translating Darwin for the historian's use.

Most historians, looking for scientific sanction for their more conventional, limited studies of narrow segments of the past, did not have to appeal to Comte, Darwin, the new physics, or theorists' dreams of either the German or American forests. They found their standard bearer in the great German historian Leopold von Ranke. American historians who had flocked to German universities had been profoundly impressed by the scientific rigor of the historical criticism practiced in seminars and so eloquently embodied in the writings of Ranke. When they returned to America they enthusiastically established their own seminars on the German plan, as had Henry Adams at Harvard and Herbert Baxter Adams at Johns Hopkins.

> There the student appears, [the latter explained] fortified by books and documents borrowed from the university library, and prepared with his brief of points and citations, like a lawyer about to plead a case in the court room. . . . Authorities are discussed; parallel sources of information are cited; old opinions are exploded; standard histories are riddled by criticism, and new values are established. This process of destruction and re-

10. "The Problem of the West," in *The Frontier in American History* (New York, Henry Holt, 1921), pp. 206, 216.

construction requires considerable literary apparatus, and the professor's study-table is usually covered with many evidences of the battle of books.[11]

The idealization of Ranke was almost a mystique among some historians. After his death in 1886 one of his American students persuaded a wealthy book collector to purchase Ranke's library, including his portrait, study table, chairs, and pens, to be contributed, as a memorial in the New World, to Syracuse University.[12] What properly impressed American historians was Ranke's disdain of pious or literary flourishes and embellishments of his narrative, his laborious research in primary sources, and his critical cross-examination of testimony. Not content with these teachings alone, many American historians saw in Ranke the high priest of a "scientific" history which would be devoted to the pursuit of isolated facts. From the hazardous enterprise of searching for generalizations and laws the historian was to turn, with new peace of mind, to the cultivation of his own garden of historical facts. In this humble refuge he could find scientific status as well as security. This was the gospel of scientific history as preached by George Burton Adams of Yale, when addressing his colleagues in 1909 as president of the American Historical Association.

In common with his contemporaries Adams revered the ideal of scientific law and believed that historical events were determined by forces acting according to fixed laws, similar to those at work in the physical sciences. Yet he deplored the defensive position of the historian faced with the aggressive rise of social scientists determined to discover these laws, and he saw no imminent possibility of the historian becoming a successful rival in this pursuit. Meanwhile, then, he could find his place by resisting the "allurements of specu-

11. "Seminary Libraries and University Extension," *Johns Hopkins University Studies in History and Political Science*, 5 (1887), 445.

12. Charles W. Bennett, "The Ranke Library in America," American Historical Association, *Papers*, 3 (1889), 131–3.

lation" and laying the factual foundations on which later thinkers
might build, for "at the very beginning of all conquest of the un-
known lies the fact, established and classified to the fullest extent
possible at the moment." Proposing the leadership of Ranke,
Adams warned: "None of the new battle-cries should sound for us
above the call of our first leader, proclaiming the chief duty of the
historian to establish *wie es eigentlich gewesen* . . . The field of the
historian is, and must long remain, the discovery and recording of
what actually happened."[13]

This clarion call massed American historians behind the German's
banner, but the leader they hailed bore little resemblance to the real
Ranke, who had been led to the study of history by philosophical
and religious interests, had preferred to lecture on general history
rather than on narrow topics, and had thought of the historical fact
as "something which is, on the outside, merely a particular thing,
but in its essence is something general with a meaning and a spirit."[14]
Throughout his career Ranke had worked toward a theory of historical forces as ideas which focused moral energies divine in origin.
He was much closer to the German tradition of idealism, which had
always challenged the dominance and arrogance of the positivistic
spirit, than any of his American disciples, who worshiped so un-
critically at the shrine of science. They had simply made Ranke over
in their own image. It was during the prevalence of this positivistic
mood that one prominent American historian argued for the
Americanization of immigrants by filling their minds with facts of
American history, which, though they might not understand them,
they had to take like medicine; while another distinguished scholar

13. "History and the Philosophy of History," *AHR*, *14* (1909), 236. For a
good exposition of "scientific history" see W. Stull Holt, "The Idea of
Scientific History in America," *Journal of History of Ideas*, *1* (1940), 352–62.

14. Quoted by Edward Gaylord Bourne, *Essays in Historical Criticism* (New
York, Charles Scribner's Sons, 1901), pp. 256–7. See also Ernst Cassirer, *The
Problem of Knowledge*, trans. W. H. Woglom and C. W. Hendel (New Haven,
Yale University Press, 1950), esp. p. 234.

affirmed that "the truest form of historical expression was the bare statement of fact in bald language."[15] With some historians the fetish of fact and the lure of law had equal attraction. Edward Cheyney, for example, contended at one time that "the simple but arduous task of the historian was to collect facts, view them objectively, and arrange them as the facts themselves demanded, without reference to any especial operating force beyond that clearly shown by actual conditions." Yet later, in his presidential address to the American Historical Association, Cheyney described man as part of a law-controlled world, formulated six laws of history, and held forth the promise that if we knew the laws of history "we might reason and act with the same intelligence and precision and anticipation of success with which the engineer acts in conformity with the known laws of physics."[16]

This American brand of historical positivism was challenged by a new movement, anticipated by Frederick Jackson Turner, publicized by James Harvey Robinson and Harry Elmer Barnes, and known as the New History. In the same year that Turner had publicly proposed his famous hypothesis about the central role of the frontier in American development he also had published in an obscure journal an important manifesto entitled "The Significance of History." This eloquent credo, which vibrates with a deeply felt devotion to historical studies, has been neglected because of the contemporary controversy over his frontier theory. Insufficient attention has therefore been given to his philosophical ideas, which anticipate both the relativism and antiformalism later developed by Becker and Beard. Turner's views directly challenged the static ideal of historical truth implied by the American disciples of Ranke, as well as their naïve ideal of fact-finding as the essence of scientific

15. Edward Channing, "Justin Winsor," *AHR, 3* (1898), 201. For John B. McMaster on the use of history in Americanizing foreigners see "The Meeting of the American Historical Association at Chicago," *AHR, 10* (1905), 497.

16. Cf. "Proceedings," American Historical Association, *Annual Report, 1* (1901), 29, with "Law in History," *AHR, 29* (1924), 247–8.

method. *Each age* (Turner wrote, foreshadowing key concepts of Becker and Beard) *writes the history of the past anew with reference to the conditions uppermost in its own time.*[17] If economic history was becoming increasingly important in the modern world, that was because historians lived in an age of factories and machines. Following the German historian Droysen, Turner saw history as "the self-consciousness of the living age acquired by understanding its development from the past," and he taught that the student's first lesson was to discard the notion that there were "standard ultimate histories." There were no last words, only the most recent efforts of society to understand itself in the light of its past.[18] In his presidential address to his fellow historians in 1910 Turner chastized the followers of Ranke:

> Those who insist that history is simply the effort to tell the thing exactly as it was, to state the facts, are confronted with the difficulty that the fact which they would represent is not planted on the solid ground of fixed conditions; it is in the midst and is itself a part of the changing currents, the complex and interacting influences of the time, deriving its significance as a fact from its relations to the deeper-seated movements of the age, movements so gradual that often only the passing years can reveal the truth about the fact and its right to a place on the historian's page.[19]

His concern for "the deeper-seated movements of the age" led Turner to branch off from the main stream of the historical writing of his time with its primary stress on political and legal institutions. His teacher, Herbert Baxter Adams, at Johns Hopkins, where the

17. *The Early Writings of Frederick Jackson Turner,* intro. Fulmer Mood (Madison, University of Wisconsin Press, 1939), p. 52.

18. Ibid., pp. 53–4.

19. "Social Forces in American History," in *The Frontier in American History,* p. 332.

motto "History is Past Politics" was carved in stone over the library door, had taught that civil society was the ground and goal of history, but Turner, in 1904, marked out a new route for historians to explore: "But behind institutions, behind constitutional forms, lie the vital forces that call these organs into life and shape them to meet changing conditions. . . . The institutional framework of a nation may be likened to the anatomy of the body politic; its physiology is the social and economic life molding this framework to new uses. Here it is that we find the field for widest study. . . . When once the investigator grasps this conception, he has found a life work, a work demanding the cooperative study of many students for generations."[20] To realize this new aim Turner, despite his own dogmatic insistence in practice on his frontier thesis, called upon historians to recognize the value of a "multiple hypothesis" approach, stemming from a broad appreciation of the contributions of other disciplines to the historian's work.

These new tendencies in historical thought found their publicists in James Harvey Robinson and Harry Elmer Barnes of Columbia University. Robinson launched the crusade for the New History with his book of that title in 1911. Explicitly rebuking George B. Adams for his appeal to Ranke, Robinson inscribed a new slogan on his banner—*wie es eigentlich geworden*. The true aim of the historian was to determine not what had happened, but how things had come about. "The present has hitherto been the willing victim of the past," said Robinson; "the time has come when it should turn on the past and exploit it in the interests of advance."[21] To use history to explain present problems was the only way the historian could avoid the dead ends of sensationalism, melodrama, or mere antiquarianism. In his search for a usable past the historian found his justification in the role played by memory in our personal

20. "Problems in American History," in *The Early Writings*, pp. 73–4.
21. "The New History," in *The New History: Essays Illustrating the Modern Historical Outlook* (New York, Harper and Bros., 1922), p. 24.

lives when "we adjust our recollection to our needs and aspirations, and ask from it light on the particular problems that face us."[22] Barnes joined Robinson in sallies against the stock character of the "orthodox historian," allegedly devoted to pedantry, politics, and hero worship. For the New Historians, unaware that Turner had reduced their whipping boy to a bugaboo, the time had come to talk of shoes and ships and sealing wax, of cabbages instead of kings. Social and economic history was the real business of the historian, who would get from the social scientists the laws necessary for making sense of his data or, failing to collaborate, be degraded to a mere field worker for the sociologist.[23]

With the blessing of the New History science and reform were to be wedded. Whereas Turner had suggested that history might "hold the lamp for conservative reform,"[24] Robinson and Barnes, like modern Savonarolas of Social Science, preached the gospel of "liberated Intelligence." Robinson's *The Mind in the Making,* a best-seller of the 1920's, was a popular plea for men to cast aside the outmoded furniture of their minds, the merely primitive residue of the animal, the savage, and the child, so that they might inhabit a rational future. Like the Enlightenment *philosophes,* the crusaders for the New History envisaged the past as a burden of error and wrong from which men were to be liberated by scientific intelligence. For all their show of scientific skepticism, Robinson and Barnes, like the *philosophes,* were devotees of their own religion of progress. Robinson, in a tone of almost pulpit unction, identified "the long-disputed sin against the Holy Ghost" as "the refusal to cooperate with the vital principle of betterment"; and Barnes, like a 20th-century Voltaire attacking the infamy of superstition, warned

22. "History for the Common Man," ibid., pp. 134–5.

23. *The New History and the Social Studies* (New York, Century, 1925), p. 329.

24. "Social Forces in American History," in *The Frontier in American History,* pp. 323–4.

that if the extension of scientific control over society was impossible, then "the 'jig is up' with the human race."[25]

If the New History was neither so new nor so historical as some of its crusaders believed, it was, nevertheless, an important part of Becker's and Beard's climate of opinion. As a graduate student at the University of Wisconsin, Becker had sat at the feet of the true father of the movement. "To me, nothing can be duller than historical facts," he wrote Turner in 1910, "and nothing more interesting than the service they can be made to render in the effort to solve the everlasting riddle of human existence. It is from you, my dear Professor Turner, more than from anyone else, that I have learned to distinguish historical facts from their uses."[26] Not only had the brilliant example of Turner inspired Becker to become a historian, but the frontier thesis, with its bleak implication that American democracy had been a function of a passing economic stage, was a vital strain in his own mature thinking. For his part, Beard, though critical of Turner's single-minded stress on the frontier, gladly acknowledged him as a pioneer in the study of economic group-conflicts—a field that Beard later made his own. Both Becker and Beard had close contacts with the Columbia spokesmen for the New History. Becker had done graduate work under Robinson, whom he later praised for his teaching that studying history "objectively," in the style of the Ranke disciples, meant studying it "without an object," but he twitted Barnes on his tilting at the windmills of "orthodoxy" by remarking that the New History was at least as old as Voltaire, while one of Barnes' own books on

25. Robinson, "The Spirit of Conservatism in the Light of History," in *The New History*, p. 265; Barnes, "James Harvey Robinson," in *American Masters of Social Science*, ed. Howard Odum, American Social Science Series (New York, Holt, 1927), p. 405. For Robinson's view of history as a compendium of errors see his *The Mind in the Making: The Relation of Intelligence to Social Reform* (New York, Harper and Bros., 1921) and his "The Newer Ways of Historians," *AHR*, 35 (1930), 245–55.

26. Letter (draft), May 15, 1910, Becker Papers.

the World War dealt entirely with political, military, and diplomatic events and highly exaggerated the role of individuals in the historical process, just as if it had been the product of an "orthodox historian."[27] Beard, on the other hand, if farther removed from Turner's influence, was closer to the New History. As a professor of Politics at Columbia and a lecturer at The New School for Social Research, Beard was a friend and colleague of both Robinson and Barnes. He had, in fact, collaborated with Robinson to produce a history text which, in New History fashion, aimed to explain the present by the past and ended with the characteristic prophecy that "it may well be that men of science, not kings, or warriors, or even statesmen are to be the heroes of the future."[28]

In their revolt against the disciples of Ranke, their linkage of history and reform, and their confidence in the promise of liberation through scientific intelligence, all of these practitioners of the New History stood on common ground. Yet Becker and Beard, though stimulated by this movement and a part of it, were skeptics who, rather than spreading the good news of any gospel, preferred to raise questions that unsettled the very foundations of historical inquiry. In their radical questioning of conventional conceptions they had an ally in pragmatism, the major philosophical influence of their time. William James had given a new importance to history in his attack against "the block universe" of both mechanism and rationalism. He proposed in opposition to all closed systems the vision of an unfinished, growing, adventuresome world. The mind was no passive re-echoing of the environment; it was always an active, selective fighter for particular ends, whether operating as attention, sensation, or reasoning. "Our thoughts," he wrote, "determine our acts, and our acts redetermine the previous nature of the world."[29] He protested against the "stagnant felicity" of Josiah Royce's om-

27. "What Is Historiography?" *AHR*, *44* (1938), 23.
28. *The Development of Modern Europe* (New York, Ginn, 1907–08), *2*, 421.
29. *A Pluralistic Universe* (New York, Longmans Green, 1909), pp. 317–18.

niscient and perfect Absolute: "I am finite once for all, and all the categories of my sympathy are knit up with the finite world *as such,* and with things that have a history."[30] Allied with James in his challenging of the traditional absolutes, John Dewey taught that metaphysical problems were solvable only when the organism was seen to be in nature "not as marbles are in a box but as events are in a history, in a moving, growing never finished process."[31] He, too, revolted against "the spectator theory of knowledge" with its conception of a "pure reason" passively contemplating fixed essences. Man's search for truth, controlled by his practical will, was an effort to adjust himself to a hazardous environment, a purpose to be measured in terms of future, active, practical consequences. In his *Logic: The Theory of Inquiry* Dewey devoted only a few pages to the implications of pragmatism for historical knowledge. Becker and Beard would, at least, have found familiar Dewey's argument that "changes going on in the present, giving a new turn to social problems, throw the significance of what happened in the past into a new perspective." They would have heartily assented, too, when Dewey spoke of an intelligent understanding of past history as "a lever for moving the present into a certain kind of future."[32]

If Becker and Beard were not pragmatists in any technical sense, they shared a pragmatic voluntarism, oriented toward the future. Becker's notes on *A Pluralistic Universe* show that he felt James' picture of experience as a dynamic "going concern" destroyed any final absolutes, and Beard praised pragmatism as the only philosophy in harmony with American life and culture. Yet they were not mere disciples. Becker said that a reading of Dewey had only confirmed a "native tendency" toward pragmatism, and Beard la-

30. Ibid., p. 48.

31. *The Philosophy of John Dewey,* comp. and ed. Joseph Ratner (New York, Holt, 1928), p. 81.

32. *Logic: The Theory of Inquiry* (New York, Holt, 1938), pp. 238–9.

mented that it had never worked out a theory of history.[33] What they both had in common with pragmatism was not so much a doctrine as a temper of mind: a secular spirit, a belief in the relevance of time and circumstance to truth and value, an involvement with modern social problems, a desire to link science with reform, a confidence in technological progress, and, above all, a sense of the primacy of the practical will.

Since James and Dewey did not make a central problem out of history, as either inquiry or action, Becker and Beard naturally looked to European thinkers for help. Yet they scanned these foreign philosophies with an alien and eclectic eye and often saw in them only the reflected image of their own purposes, shaped by an American tradition. The basic ideas of these two historians must be understood against the background of the American development of historical thought, from the cult of "laws" or "facts" to the crusade for the New History. It is this climate of opinion that conditioned and provoked their own revision of their tradition.

Both Becker and Beard called upon the historian to cast off the chains which bound him to the idol of science. The scientific historians had distorted the purpose, method, and value of historical inquiry. They had failed to recognize the radically humanistic quality of their subject. Their pretensions had, above all, blinded them to a realization that the historian is necessarily a participant in the very process he studies. Neither he nor his writings can escape history. In thus reorienting the philosophy of history in America, Becker and Beard developed a new theory which critics have labeled "subjectivist-relativist-presentism." This ugly terminology—though my own phrase of "skeptical" or "pragmatic" relativism may not seem less barbarous—expresses the belief that Becker and Beard

33. For Becker see "Miscellaneous," Notes, drawer 15, Becker Papers; and Malcolm Cowley, "Books That Changed Our Minds," *New Republic, 97* (December 7, 1938), 135. For Beard see Charles A. and Mary R. Beard, *The American Spirit: A Study of the Idea of Civilization in the United States,* Vol. 4 of The Rise of American Civilization (New York, Macmillan, 1942), p. 670.

fatally undermined the historian's confidence that he can tell the historical truth about the past. The code of the scientific historian may have been naïve; it may even have been oppressive; but it was at least a code. Becker and Beard failed to make clear just what new responsibilities the historian assumes when he no longer pretends to be a scientist. The ironic truth is, as the next two chapters attempt to make clear, their revolution was not radical enough. They succumbed in the end to positivism.

CHAPTER TWO

Everyman His Own Historian

CARL BECKER'S humane and skeptical intelligence was genuinely Socratic in its inability to be satisfied with the common and crude abstractions most people accepted for self-evident truths. He went to a dictionary, he said, to find out what unfamiliar words meant, but when he had to use words "with which everyone is perfectly familiar," he decided "the wise thing to do is to take a week off and think about them."[1] As early as 1910 he began to exercise his talent for gentle, ironic deflation on the self-evident truths of the scientific historians with their "laws of history," their "cold, hard facts," and their "objective detachment." Displaying a sophistication and subtlety all too rare among historians, he exposed the superficial thinking that had created these abstractions. He did such a devastating job that it is hard to believe that anyone with an intellectual conscience can ever revive them again in their old meaning without wincing, even though he may rightly feel that Becker's own theory is far from adequate as a philosophy of history.

Becker's search for a philosophical approach to history was not a quest, in the spirit of Henry Adams, for some formula to sum up the whole sweep of historical events.[2] It was, instead, an attempt to

1. "What Are Historical Facts?" *Western Political Quarterly, 8* (1955), 328. This article is a reprinting of Becker's address to the American Historical Association at Rochester in 1926.

2. For Becker's explanation of Adams' personal need to seek a science of history see the two essays on Adams in *Everyman His Own Historian: Essays on History and Politics* (New York, Appleton Century Crofts, 1935), pp. 143–68.

see the historian and his subject in finite, human terms. Adams'
theory, expressed in the terminology of physics, seemed to Becker
an irrelevant piece of dubious speculation. History, he felt, must be
written from the human and not from the cosmic point of view,
even if the cosmos itself is utterly indifferent to man's doings. Man's
doings are interesting and important to himself, measured by human
purposes, whether or not history is ultimately headed for either
"the ash-heap or the millennium." The historian's proper interest,
he felt, is the sphere of "finite and human values and meaning,"[3]
as these are revealed in man's thought and action. From the stand-
point of a cosmic intelligence, for whom there are no values except
form, extension, and velocity, man's "imperishable monuments"
and "immortal deeds" may appear infinitesimal, impotent, and irrelevant. But, in fact, there is no such cosmic intelligence. Man
alone can view both himself and the cosmos. Of his insignificance
in the cosmos the cosmos knows nothing. The cosmic view of man's
fate in an indifferent universe, running down, is itself a product of
man's scientific intelligence—"the manifestation of his insatiable
curiosity, his indefeasible determination to know." As such, Becker
argued, it is less "an objective world of fact than man's creation of
the world in his own image."[4]

The historian and the scientist, he felt, have different objectives.
For one the discovery of impersonal laws is appropriate, because
science is concerned with the repeatable, the recurring, and the
abstract; for the other the pursuit of such laws is meaningless because
the historian's interest lies in the specific character of an actual concrete situation. The value of science is its power to predict what
will happen under given conditions. "The value of history is, indeed, not scientific but moral: by liberalizing the mind, by deepen-
ing the sympathies, by fortifying the will, it enables us to control,

3. Review of Henry Adams, *The Degradation of the Democratic Dogma,* in
AHR, 25 (1920), 482. Cf. "Mr. Wells and the New History," in *Everyman
His Own Historian,* p. 181.
4. *Progress and Power* (Stanford, Stanford University Press, 1936), p. 102.

not society, but ourselves,—a much more important thing; it pre-
pares us to live more humanely in the present and to meet rather
than to foretell the future."[5] Abstract knowledge of the impersonal
processes of behavior may, Becker admitted, be sufficient for the
student of beetles; but as men are not beetles, the historian dealing
with the problem of Socrates sitting in his prison cell, for example,
needs to know why the Athenians condemned him and why he
saw fit to accept their punishment. It is no help to the historian,
trying to explain why Socrates was sitting there in prison, to analyze
the processes of physiology that make such posture possible.[6] There
is, after all, a difference between man and the atom: the atom cannot
have a knowledge of physics. Deterministic theories of history fail
to account for the role of man's knowledge in making history.
"Only man has a history," Becker believed, "in the sense that his
own knowledge (or what he accepts as knowledge) of the history
of all things, including himself, is an essential factor in determining
what his own objective history has been and will be."[7] To look at
man through the eyes of science alone is to objectify him and de-
prive him of his power of self-criticism. Becker himself was once
dismissed by a Marxist historian as a middle-class intellectual who
could not hope to understand the proletarian nature of the American
Revolution. With pointed irony Becker refused to reply to this
criticism on the ground that "as an object for methodical examination," like an electron exposed to light, it was his part, obviously,
"to look natural when posed as an object interesting to science, to
remain indifferent and undeflected," so long as there was any call
for his services "as a datum in sociology."[8]

The last refuge of the image of the historian as scientist was the

5. "A New Philosophy of History," *Dial,* 59 (1915), 148.
6. Review of Frederick J. Teggart, *The Processes of History,* in *AHR, 24*
(1919), 267–8.
7. "The Function of the Social Sciences," in *Science and Man,* ed. Ruth
Nanda Anshen (New York, Harcourt Brace, 1942), p. 245.
8. "The Subjective Object and Vice Versa," *New Republic 85* (1936), 256.

school of Ranke followers. It sought for historians the prestige of science in the simple ascertainment of fact. The historian could preserve his neutral objectivity in his function of relating "what actually happened." Becker began his campaign against this version of historical knowledge in 1910 (only a year after George B. Adams had raised the flag of Ranke) with an article entitled "Detachment and the Writing of History," appearing in a popular monthly. The position he took here, though developed and refined in more technical papers presented at a 1912 meeting of the American Sociological Society and at a session of the American Historical Association in 1926, clearly anticipated his famous presidential address to the historical guild in 1931, "Everyman His Own Historian." From these four sources the architecture of Becker's historical theory can be constructed.

Becker began by trying to shatter the naïve confidence of the Ranke-inspired historians in "cold, hard facts." Instead of being external, clearly defined, objective things, historical facts are, he argued, mental realities. Not all past events are historical, only those which have made some difference because they have been remembered, thus becoming a part of human experience: "It is the persisting historical fact, rather than the ephemeral actual event, which makes a difference to us now; and the historical fact makes a difference only because it is, and so far as it is, in human minds."[9] Because the historical fact has been remembered, it can be recorded; because it has been recorded, it can become available to the historian, for no past sequence of events is presently observable. The historian's facts, strictly speaking, are his conclusions derived from analyzing documents. He does not produce a past event, "but a symbol which enables us to recreate it imaginatively."[10] Historical facts have, then, a twofold mental life: they live, first, in the minds of those who have chosen to record them and, second, in the minds

9. "What Are Historical Facts?" p. 332.
10. Ibid., p. 330.

of those who have analyzed the records. No doubt some events have no life in the minds of either the past authors of documents or the present students of them, but these events are not *historical* facts, as Becker defined them.

Ranke's adherents made the further mistake, Becker felt, of assuming that history could be described atomistically in terms of separate, self-contained facts, like marbles in a box. That Caesar was stabbed by senators in the senate house of Rome is, Becker argued, a simple statement of fact only in the sense that the sentence can be easily understood. It is not, however, a statement of simple fact, but a simple statement of complex fact which includes "the senators standing round, the words that were said, the scuffle, the three and twenty dagger-strokes—numberless facts, indeed, make the single fact that Caesar was stabbed in the senate-house." Becker concluded: "Thus, while we speak of historical facts as if they were pebbles to be gathered in a cup, there is in truth no unit fact in history."[11] It is not the isolated particularity of events that makes them meaningful for the historian; on the contrary, they are meaningful only because they play a role in a web of relationships. The statement that Caesar crossed the Rubicon, or was killed in the senate, is significant only as "a symbol standing for a long series of events which have to do with the most intangible and immaterial realities, viz.: the relations between Caesar and the millions of people of the Roman world."[12] Conventional views of the historian's analysis of testimony implied that his duty is simply to collect all the statements of reliable witnesses about past events. Not only does the wealth of evidence make this chore impossible, Becker pointed out, but even if it could be done, the historian would, "by submerging and suffocating the mind in diffuse existence, accomplish the superfluous task of depriving human experience of all significance."[13] History

11. "Detachment and the Writing of History," *Atlantic, 106* (1910), 527.
12. "What Are Historical Facts?" p. 329.
13. "Everyman His Own Historian," in *Everyman His Own Historian*, pp. 250–1.

as the lifeless knowledge of whatever happens to have happened is meaningless. Even the simplest fact of the historian must have some place in a pattern of ideas: "To set forth historical facts is not comparable to dumping a barrow of bricks."[14]

Because of their superficial conception of the nature of historical facts, Ranke's followers supported an equally naïve theory of historical objectivity. History to them, as Becker remarked, was like a solid, material thing, "much as if the facts of history were a number of blocks which had fallen down; which might be set up again; and which, once set up in the order, precisely, in which they had originally stood, would spell out an intelligible word."[15] This view presupposed that the original pattern is clearly indicated by the blocks themselves. Since "facts speak for themselves," the historian has only to keep all subjective elements out of his work. This dogma puts a ban not only on bias and prejudice but on explanation and evaluation as well. For all their devotion to science, as a guide for the historian, the devotees of Ranke failed to understand what the natural scientist himself does in his investigation of nature. They believed that history, like nature, would utter its secrets by confession without any cross-examination. Yet it was Francis Bacon, one of the great philosophers of scientific method, who spoke, in the phraseology of the lawyer, of the necessity for "putting Nature to the question."[16] In their distrust of philosophical speculation these historians had submitted to the philosophy that, in Becker's phrase, by not taking thought, a cubit would be added to their stature: "Hoping to find something without looking for it, expecting to obtain final answers to life's riddle by resolutely refusing to ask

14. Ibid., p. 251.

15. "Some Aspects of the Influence of Social Problems and Ideas upon the Study and Writing of History," *Publications of the American Sociological Society*, 7 (1913), 93–4.

16. R. G. Collingwood, *The Idea of History* (Oxford, Oxford University Press, 1946), p. 269. See also Morris R. Cohen, *The Meaning of Human History* (La Salle, Ill., Open Court, 1947), pp. 204–5.

questions—it was surely the most romantic species of realism yet invented, the oddest attempt ever made to get something for nothing!"[17]

This image of the mind as a passive mirror of events produced a false objectivity which led historians to pride themselves on their lack of ideas, their colorless prose, and their indifference to moral judgment. Becker mocked those pseudoscientific critics who would, as he pointed out, have no doubts about the scientific standing of Francis Parkman's works if he had only written badly. The kind of objectivity that Becker admired in Turner had nothing in common with those "cultivated repressions such as would enable any careful historian to write, let us say, an account of the Battle of Cold Harbor without revealing the fact that his father was an ardent admirer of Grant." It was instead that "intense and sustained interest which an abundance of ideas can alone generate."[18] Pedestrian style and lack of imagination were bad enough, especially to a writer as witty and subtle as Becker, but even worse was the moral smugness engendered by the cult of Ranke. Interpretation of events, banned in theory, was smuggled back in by a covert identification in practice of power and righteousness. Studied "objectively," history, he feared, gave rise to the vicious doctrine that success is the evidence of right. The historian who aimed at achieving impartiality by searching for some region of safe neutrality would find it, he believed, in the most convenient place—accomplished fact: "The mere 'fact,' if you allow the wretched creature to open its mouth, will say only one thing: 'I am, therefore I am right.' "[19] This complacency was not much different from the *realpolitik* cynicism of those German historians who believed in justification by fact, accomplished through fear, favor, force, and fraud. This moral callousness, which repulsed Becker in the histories and memoirs justi-

17. "Everyman His Own Historian," p. 250.
18. "Frederick Jackson Turner," ibid., pp. 208-9.
19. "A Chronicle of Facts," *New Republic*, 25 (1921), 382. Cf. "German Historians and the Great War, " *Dial, 60* (1916), 163.

fying Germany's role in the first World War, seemed to him to have its roots in the idolization of Ranke. The success of Bismarck's policy of "blood and iron" had fostered the identification of might and right, not only among statesmen but among historians as well.

Becker's analysis of the process of historical synthesis marked his most radical break with the tradition of scientific history. The view of objectivity as passive detachment implied "a dead mind, lying among the facts of history like unmagnetized steel among iron-filings, no synthesis ever resulting . . . to the end of time."[20] Yet even those who recognized that facts had to be organized into complexes of facts were somehow confident of securing an ultimate agreement on synthesis that would be accepted by scientific historians everywhere. This confidence in the universal truth of historical narratives seemed to him to rest on a circular argument. The selection of facts, they said, is not arbitrary because facts are chosen for their structural importance in a whole, or complex pattern of facts; yet, if facts are chosen on this basis, the historian has to know what the whole is before he selects his facts to compose it. But if he knows the whole before he selects his facts, how can his synthesis be based on the facts? To this dilemma, as proposed by Becker, one historical theorist of the day simply answered: "When the evidence is all in, the problem of what the whole is and what facts are important for the whole has been solved in a rough way."[21] For Becker the solution was much too rough, for when and how can it be determined that all the evidence is in without some conception of the limits of the inquiry? The distressing situation for the historian, he pointed out, is that a total grasp of all the facts is impossible:

> If we had all the data of all events, and a mind capable of grasping the data in their actual relations, everything would be im-

20. "Detachment and the Writing of History," *Atlantic*, 106 (1910), 534.

21. Fred Morrow Fling, *The Writing of History: An Introduction to Historical Method* (New Haven, Yale University Press, 1920), p. 132. For Becker's critique of Fling see "Detachment and the Writing of History," p. 531.

mediately understood and immediately pardoned. In this timeless existence there would be no occasion for "views," no
occasion for distinctions between facts and non-facts, facts and
interpretations, meaning and non-meaning, good and bad,
being and becoming: everything would simply be, the entire
blest *wie es eigentlich gewesen sei* would just be there and nothing
to write home about. We would have the Truth, and the Truth
would make us free, free to do nothing—except sit and contemplate the Truth.[22]

Becker's answer to the problem of synthesis led him to the
skeptical relativism that has made him such a controversial figure.
He urged the historian to accept for his own field the implications
of pragmatism, which made truth and reality subject to change.
Did not pragmatism, he asked, undercut the Olympian ideal of
objectivity, "based upon the familiar conception of the 'pure
reason'—reason cut loose from will and emotion, from purpose and
passion, and desire . . ."?[23] It was necessary, he felt, to analyze the
process of historical reconstruction in the light of this new outlook.
From this point of view one must start with the premise that to
read testimony on the past the historian has to supply out of his own
experience the elements by which a picture of the past is drawn. To
know that Caesar was assassinated, he must also know about men,
senate rooms, and daggers. Becker admitted that new sources of
knowledge from the past help the historian to combine the elements
of his experience more correctly: reading more about the Roman
senate keeps him from assuming it was the Senate in Washington.
But unless experience is brought to the documents, they remain
mere pieces of paper with strange marks on them. Present experience, furthermore, is, he maintained, the last court of appeals in
evaluating testimony. Past testimony cannot establish as a reality

22. Review of Maurice Mandelbaum, *The Problem of Historical Knowledge*,
in *Philosophical Review*, *49* (1940), 363-4.
23. "Detachment and the Writing of History," p. 527.

something the historian knows to be impossible on the basis of his present experience. Thus a cloud of witnesses cannot make miracles be facts if present scientific experience repudiates miracles. By analogy, he argued, for a modern mind, aware of economics and psychology as sciences, the medieval monasteries and Stylites on his pillar would be understood not as expressions of religious faith but as episodes in the class struggle and pathology.[24]

The historian's selection of facts and their interconnections, in Becker's theory, depends both on the prevailing scientific conceptions and on the historian's personal presuppositions, values, and outlook, which are, in turn, historical products of the social forces of his age. William James had shown in his analysis of "the specious present" of the individual's "stream of consciousness" that "the practically cognized present is no knife-edge, but a saddle-back, with a certain breadth of its own on which we sit perched, and from which we look in two directions into time."[25] The New History movement had stressed the way in which men adjusted their memories to their needs when seeking light on their problems. In "Everyman His Own Historian" Becker elaborated an argument that resembles these ideas of James and Robinson. The value of history, Becker believed, is its enlargement and enrichment of "the specious present" so that men may know what they are doing in the light of what they have done and hope to do. Like Mr. Everyman who, wanting to pay his coal bill, researches his account books, the historian studies only those things which can be related with relevance and harmony to his own activities as a member of society. Being neither omniscient nor omnipresent, the historian, like "the wise man of the tribe," gives to remembered and memorable events a varied form and significance. In this process, as with Mr. Everyman himself, memory of the past and anticipation of the future go hand in hand. The successful historian, who creates the kind of living

24. Ibid., pp. 528 ff.

25. William James, *The Principles of Psychology* (London, Macmillan, 1891), 1, 609.

history that influences the course of history, enlarges and enriches not just his own consciousness but "the collective specious present, the specious present of Mr. Everyman." The historian, in the end, does not impose his version of the human story on Mr. Everyman; it is rather Mr. Everyman "who imposes his version on us—compelling us, in an age of political revolution, to see that history is past politics, in an age of social stress and conflict to search for the economic interpretation."[26] The historian, being a part of the process he studies, cannot escape changing with it: "The past is a kind of screen upon which we project our vision of the future; and it is indeed a moving picture, borrowing much of its form and color from our fears and aspirations."[27] The historian's interpretations are part of an evolution in which only the fittest survive, and to qualify for survival they must conform to the collective "specious present" of Mr. Everyman. In this sense Becker believed with Voltaire that history is "a pack of tricks we play on the dead." To the dogmatism of the scientific school Becker had opposed a fundamental skepticism.

He had the courage of his lack of conviction in the fixity of truth. He did not present even his own relativism as a stable theory that must prevail: "Whatever validity it may claim, it is certain, on its own premises, to be supplanted; for its premises, imposed upon us by the climate of opinion in which we live and think, predispose us to regard all things, and all principles of things, as no more than 'inconstant modes or fashions,' as but the 'concurrence, renewed from moment to moment, of forces parting sooner or later on their way.' "[28] If his tone seemed at times like that of a jesting Pilate who would not stay for an answer ("O History, how many truths have been committed in thy name!"[29]), it was partly because he had a

26. "Everyman His Own Historian," p. 253.
27. "What Are Historical Facts?" p. 337.
28. "Everyman His Own Historian," p. 254.
29. "Mr. Wells and the New History," in *Everyman His Own Historian,* p. 169.

teasing wit, designed to prod the dogmatic slumbers of the scientific historians. Yet even Becker himself recognized that his theory bordered upon nihilism. Relativism, as he said, "without metaphysical foundation, is likely to issue in a skeptical disillusionment, the conviction that all thought is no more than a pragmatic instrument employed by the animal man in his effort to find warm corners in a cold universe."[30] By 1944, challenged and alarmed by the rise of fascist irrationalism, he came to feel that the strength of democracy was its concern for the impulse to know what is *true* and its effort to build civilization on *verifiable* knowledge.[31] Perhaps, if he had not died in 1945, he would have been able to revise his theory in the light of this new emphasis.

A just appraisal of Becker must begin with an appreciation of his demolition work on the rickety structure of scientific history. He punctured the inflated pretensions of deterministic theories of history which assumed that the historical process could be understood from outside in some cosmic perspective. He awoke historians to the realization that science and history have different objectives and values. He disabused them of the fallacy that there is a fixed and finished past, still standing in some ghostly limbo, clearly visible to a spectator, as if the historian were a sightseer alighting from a time-machine that had carried him back into the past. He pointed instead to the central role of the historian as an active present participant in human experience, trying to enlarge and enrich his perspective by linking himself to the thought and action of life in the past. In these respects Becker contributed to the progressive development of American historical thought.

Yet his conclusions have understandably alarmed his critics. His emphasis on present social needs and hopes, as determining factors in historical judgment, as well as his seeming mockery of any kind

30. Review of A. N. Whitehead, *Adventures in Ideas,* in *AHR, 39* (1933), 89.
31. "Learning and the Life of Man," in *Return to Freedom,* ed. Thomas H. Johnson (New York, G. P. Putnam's Sons, 1944), p. 22.

of historical truth or objectivity both threaten to dissolve the distinction between history and propaganda, knowledge and myth. If Becker began by defending the claims of value against those of fact, he ended by resolving all standards of value, including the historian's, into the contemporary flux of social forces. Written history was only "the specious present" of the historian writ large, and "the specious present" of the historian was only that of Mr. Everyman's writ small. The historian, from this point of view, becomes the rationalizer of the collective social consciousness of the day, fabricating a useful past.

Becker himself was gifted with a powerful historical imagination which he exercised with unusual sophistication in his probings of the climate of opinion which prevailed in a past age. It was precisely for this reason that he was sensitive to the ways in which written history had itself fulfilled some need of an earlier climate of opinion. He was fascinated, above all, in the use men had made of their beliefs about the past to advance their social aspirations. The historian's *sense* of the past, not his verifiable knowledge about it, made written history itself a part of actual history. To study the writings of past historians the historiographer had to cultivate "a capacity for imaginative understanding."[32] What Becker then did was to generalize upon his own discoveries of the way in which written histories had played a functional role in past societies: every historical synthesis was a function of the social needs and aspirations of the time in which it was made. This conclusion placed him in a dilemma which he never fully comprehended: the integrity of the capacity for imaginative understanding, which enabled Becker to see the past historian as part of the historical process, is itself destroyed if the present historian is *only* an illustration of his contemporary climate of opinion. For how, then, could Becker achieve that indispensable imaginative understanding of the past if he was doomed to see the past only through the distorting spectacles of his

32. "What Is Historiography?" *AHR, 44* (1938), 22.

own age? Relativism thus produced a contradiction in historical thought: if the historian is time-locked in the prison of his own climate of opinion, he cannot give a historical account of the outside world.

As a practicing historian, Becker knew that to study history is always to attempt a self-transcendence that makes possible an imaginative grasp of men whose purposes are not our own and whose world seems at first alien and unintelligible. Yet he propounded a theory that did not account for this power of imaginative understanding he so richly possessed. This omission, fatal to the adequacy of his position, is eloquent testimony to Becker's ambiguous relation to historical positivism. His skepticism was rooted in his definition of the historian's mind as a kind of social stream of consciousness, mixing memory and desire in response to the hopes and fears of society. This description dissolves the mind into the pragmatic context of the conflict of social forces and fails to give adequate recognition to the power of reflection to concentrate on intellectual and theoretical problems. If the mind can never secure even a temporary detachment from the pressures of action, which nurture hopes and fears, then natural science itself would be impossible. The mind's power to set itself critical standards of procedure and judgment is necessary for all systematic inquiry, and even Becker did not deny the intellectual responsibility and authority of scientific thought. This power of independent reflection is presupposed even by the attempt to limit the mind to nothing but a stream of consciousness: a mere stream of consciousness in perpetual flux could not achieve the detachment and objectivity required to define itself. The authority of thought can be denied only by a dogmatic determinism which makes man a mere fact in a law-controlled world, an outlook far more appropriate to the scientific historians than to one of their most brilliant critics.

Ironically, in view of his polemic against scientific history, Becker unconsciously revived in a new disguise the fallacy of the spectator theory of knowledge which he had once exposed. For him the historian's mind was, in the end, also a passive mirror, reflecting not the "cold, hard facts" of the past, certainly, but, instead, the dominant social forces of the day. But if inquiry is not passive with respect to historical evidence, neither is it passive with respect to the hopes and fears, the climate of opinion, or the social conflicts of the day. The historian's spirit of rational criticism is not limited to documents alone; it also enters into his relationship to his own time. Becker failed to smash the mirror completely. He was right to point out that the historian is dependent upon his present world for his evidence, his conceptual tools of analysis, and his problems. In this respect there is no difference between the scientist and the historian. Nor does the dependence destroy objectivity, for the present experience relevant is the intellectual world of critical thought, not the practical world of action. On this point he could have learned something from Croce, with whom he is often and mistakenly paired. As Croce argued, the pressure of the problems of the practical world of action affects the historian by creating his need for the perspective and orientation which historical understanding can provide; but this understanding itself is an act of knowledge, the solution of a particular theoretical difficulty. If thought and will are identified, the pursuit of truth is debased by practical aims, and action is deprived of the necessary guidance of knowledge. In giving such dangerous primacy to the practical will, Becker was even more pragmatic than pragmatism itself, inasmuch as Dewey accepted the dictum about telling the event "exactly as it happened" as a valuable warning against bias and took it for granted that historical reconstructions, though requalifying what exists, must meet the conditions of all authentic inquiry.[33] If the historian does not operate according to the same code of standards as the scientist, that is no reason for saying the historian cannot have standards appropriate to his own field, principles of procedure which are not

33. For Croce see *History as the Story of Liberty,* trans. Sylvia Sprigge (New York, W. W. Norton, 1941), pp. 41, 187; for Dewey see *Logic: The Theory of Inquiry* (New York, 1938), pp. 236–9.

mere weapons in the warfare of social conflict. Becker's assumption that history, since it is not at all like physics, is therefore peculiarly subjective and irresponsible paid an unconscious and undeserved tribute to those who had so strenuously tried to make the historian over in the image of the scientist.

Becker's pragmatism, his emphasis on the role of policy controlled by "a vision of the future" in historical reconstruction, was a reflection not only of this ambiguous response to the scientific historians but also of his equally ambiguous sympathy for the New History, with its faith in the idea of progress. Nothing could be more unhistorical than James Harvey Robinson's contempt for the past as a burden of irrationality to be cast off by a liberated Intelligence thus freed for an enthusiastic embrace of a radiant vision of a glorious future. Yet Becker, in comparing Croce's *History: Its Theory and Practice* and Robinson's *The Mind in the Making,* tipped the balance in favor of the latter.[34] This decision was more than an act of piety toward a former teacher; it expressed Becker's own tender regard for human hopes of reform. In *Progress and Power* he even attempted to provide an objective standard of historical progress in terms of man's conquest of nature through technology and science. Though he was fully aware of the uncritical and naïve tenor of Robinson's faith in the idea of progress, Becker, in a more sophisticated way, also believed that society could "by its own efforts indefinitely increase the happiness and welfare of all men—it is perhaps the one really vital faith of our day."[35]

34. "History as the Intellectual Adventure of Mankind," *New Republic, 30* (1922), 175–6.

35. "The New History," *Dial, 53* (1912), 20. This review of Robinson's *The New History* is, in my judgment, misinterpreted by Charlotte Watkins Smith, *Carl Becker: On History and the Climate of Opinion* (Ithaca, 1956), pp. 60–1. Because she exaggerates his differences with Robinson and neglects their common agreement, she criticizes me for arguing that Becker linked history and reform together. Cf. my "Historical Thought in America," *Virginia Quarterly Review, 28* (1952), 248–56, and "The Twentieth-century Enlightenment," *American Political Science Review, 49* (1955), 329–33.

Because of this religion of progress Becker was less anxious to defend the integrity of the historical imagination against tendentiousness in historical writing than he should have been. Thus he warmly praised H. G. Wells' *Outline of History* as a valuable tract for the times, though it was perfectly clear to Becker that Wells had not taken enough pains to find out why men thought it reasonable to do what they did, giving instead the impression of "telling us less about Dame History than about what is 'the trouble' with her . . . as if he took a paternal interest in the mending of her ways."[36] Becker the relativist stoutly approves of Wells as a writer of the New History, while Becker the historian cautiously reminds us that Wells is, after all, only a polemical publicist. In Becker's eyes much could be forgiven a man who, like Turner and Robinson, wanted history "to hold the lamp" for reform by exploiting the past in the interests of progress. What did it matter if the truth should make you free, if you were only free to contemplate the truth? There was a world to win.

From this point of view, "in times of pressure like the present," the historian studies the past "as something to be practically appraised in the light of ends that are thought to be desirable and attainable in the future."[37] Becker knew that this pragmatic approach was only one way of writing history, and he was well aware that he did not have the crusader's temperament. "I am one of those," he wrote a friend, "who are more interested in finding out as far as possible what men are like and how they think than in 'doing them good,' which I rationalize by saying that the way I can do them most good is to find out what they are like, what they do and why they do it and why they think it's a good thing to do it."[38] This quality of detachment was, in fact, what made him, in contrast to Wells, such a good historian; yet, ironically, his theory of knowledge, combined with his attachment to the idea of progress, led to a

36. "Mr. Wells and the New History," p. 185.
37. Ibid., p. 182.
38. Letter to Conyers Read, December 3, 1944, Becker Papers.

drastic subordination of the crucial ideal of the disinterested historical imagination.

Certainly Becker was right in arguing that the historian does not accept testimony at face value, but judges its validity in terms of his "settled convictions as to the nature of the universe and the kind of facts that can occur in it."[39] To this extent the historian's present determines his account of the past by providing him with a standard for discriminating the possible from the impossible. This standard is, however, not a matter of prejudice or fashion; it is the outgrowth of scientific and historical knowledge. What the historian must not do is interpret the *meaning* of testimony solely in the light of present standards. The idea of history entails the premise that the conventions, assumptions, and institutions of past peoples have a life and significance of their own, alien at first to the historian who, by an effort of imaginative sympathy, seeks to comprehend them. For this reason the historian must always be on guard lest contempt for those who lack his own standards and knowledge should blight his ability to understand them. If he is to understand why the Puritans hanged witches, he must set aside the ordinary conventions of his own world in order to recreate a life in which hanging witches made sense.

Becker was fond of comparing the work of the historian to Mr. Everyman's efforts to settle his coal bill by researching his accounts, but the example is not analogous because Mr. Everyman, moved by a practical purpose, never steps out of his immediate, commonsensical frame of reference. He takes for granted the entire ideal

---

39. "On Historical Evidence," MS (unpublished), Becker Papers, p. 15. This paper was first given as an address under the title of "Limitations of Testimony as a Method of Establishing Historical Facts" before a faculty group at Cornell in November 1937, and later at Princeton, March 31, 1938 (see Charlotte Watkins Smith, p. 88). The passage cited in my text is the sense in which Becker agreed that "history is, as Charles Beard says, 'an act of faith.' But then no more so than all experience." For Beard's view of the "act of faith" see my following chapter.

organization and structure of the social life in which his merely practical problems occur. What interests the historian is the form and function of a society in which coal is used and bills are paid by Mr. Everyman. The historian is, if analogies are to be made, much more like a cosmopolitan traveler in strange lands than a simple *bourgeois* paying his bills. If man can be studied historically, it is because instead of living from hand to mouth he has imparted a form to life by giving shape and significance to his spiritual energies, creating institutions for and monuments to his activities, and so developing and transforming himself by his achievements. The symbols he has created in this process are the documents and remains which make the historian's task both necessary and possible.

It is certainly essential for historians to appreciate the difficulties and complexities of their work, but Becker's relativism was a counsel of despair. He implied that because the historian cannot grasp the totality of past fact, he must begin with a synthesis, shaped by his hopes and fears, in order to control his selections from a sea of data. But the limits of the historian's inquiry are established neither by an abstract totality of facts nor by his present hopes and fears. He is guided instead by his present knowledge of previous scholarship on his problem, by the nature of his particular questions, and by the specific evidence they imply and invoke. Such inquiry will never be finally consummated so long as history, including man's knowledge of himself and his techniques for acquiring it, endures. In this limited sense relativism is inherent in the enterprise of human thought, ever generating new problems and reappraising old solutions. We may, as E. A. Robinson wrote in a poem Becker admired, smile at our predecessors because we have come after them and now occupy the stage: "Yet we shall have our darkness, even as they, / And there shall be another tale to tell."[40]

Becker had, at least partially, emancipated American historical

40. Becker pasted a clipping of Robinson's "Modernites," from which I have quoted the last two lines, on a card. Notes, drawer 2, Becker Papers.

thought from positivism. If he did so only at the price of a some-what disenchanted skepticism, it was largely because he could not overthrow the idea that intellectual responsibility and authority were the exclusive properties of natural science. Yet his contribution was of immense value. For many American historians Becker's presidential address, "Everyman His Own Historian," was an exciting liberation from old dogmas. W. Stull Holt joyously wrote Becker: "It was sacrilege against the deity, Scientific History, who has been enthroned for so long. It was treason against the profession. It was glorious. It was grand." So artful was it, concealing "the profound and devastating quality of your ideas," Holt added, that even the scientific historians "smiled as you took out their appendix—no, their backbone and other vital parts."[41] Becker had brilliantly found the weaknesses in the armor of Clio when dressed in scientific garb, preparing the ground for another assault, this time led by Charles Beard.

41. Letter, January 13, 1932, Becker Papers.

CHAPTER THREE

Written History as an Act of Faith

CHARLES BEARD first became famous for a particular interpretation of a historical event, the framing of the Constitution of the United States, and his consequent career was a bold and comprehensive effort to apply an economic interpretation of history to the whole story of the American past. Yet despite this commitment to a special version of historical truth, he had, like Becker, a persistent habit of raising skeptical questions about the authenticity of historical knowledge. His doubts made him an ally of Becker in the revolt against scientific history; ultimately they compelled revision of the economic interpretation itself. Lacking Becker's Socratic irony and subtlety, Beard was a passionate man who, to use his own analogy, found himself at home in the prophetic role of Jeremiah against the Philistines. He had a deep need for some organizing vision of the historical process as a whole, moving toward some luminous goal, and so for him the historian, instead of being a keeper of Mr. Everyman's useful myths about the past, was the prophet of a brave new world. After a provisional acceptance of Becker's relativism Beard hoped to go beyond him, to give the historian a more stable place to stand. Yet in the end Beard, too, was inhibited and crippled by the failure to emancipate himself from the very tradition he attacked.

It is not so surprising as it may first appear that a historian who believed in the historical truth of economic determinism came eventually to feel the force of a skeptical historical relativism. The New History had, of course, implied that if modern historians are interested in economic history, it is because they live in an age of factories and machines. From this point of view the theory of economic determinism may be only a reflection of present, practical interests. More significantly, Beard was drawn to an economic interpretation of history because of its emphasis on the relation between interests and ideas in politics, and for him the principle had universal implications: "Those who merely discuss policy likewise bring their interests to bear, consciously or unconsciously, and their interests, both intellectual and economic . . . are affiliated with some form of ownership or opposition to the present relations or operations of ownership."[1] If this premise is accepted, it is but a short step to the corollary that all discussion of human affairs, including the historian's, is infected with relativity. Thus Beard characteristically explained the influence of Ranke on historical thought by linking this tradition to the "outgrowth of the bureaucratization of German intelligence, a function of the servitude imposed upon business enterprise in Germany, where its development occurred late, with the aid of only a small intelligentsia and under the dominance of a military and civil bureaucracy."[2] The relativity implied in economic determinism prepared Beard for historical relativism and shaped his response to it.

To defend his right to apply an economic interpretation of history he was inevitably compelled to challenge the thesis that the historian achieves objectivity by passive fact-finding. The denial of any desire to interpret is itself an interpretation, he pointed out, a confession of bankruptcy based on the tacit assumption that "there is not even a discoverable fringe of order in the universe, that anarchy is the name for the chaos."[3] Without interpretation the writing of history must degenerate into antiquarianism, undeserving of labor, love, or the support of society. Beard felt that he had at least the merit of

1. *The Open Door at Home: A Trial Philosophy of National Interest,* collab. G. H. E. Smith (New York, Macmillan, 1935), p. 157.

2. Beard and Alfred Vagts, "Currents of Thought in Historiography," *AHR, 42* (1937), 476.

3. "Time, Technology, and the Creative Spirit in Political Science," *American Political Science Review, 21* (1927), 7.

candor in calling his study of the framers *An Economic Interpretation of the Constitution of the United States.* The reader was thereby warned that a particular explanation was being advanced. When his approach was accused of making impartiality impossible, he pointed out that conceivably the historian may "view the structure of classes, their ideologies, formulas, projects, and conflicts as coldly and impartially as any disciple of Ranke that the American Historical Association has furnished."[4]

Whatever the merits or defects of economic determinism may be, Beard was profoundly convinced that European philosophers of history, like Croce, Karl Heussi, Kurt Riezler, and Karl Mannheim, had, in the years between 1916 and 1933, forever destroyed the pretensions and authority of scientific history, whether in the spirit of Comte, Darwin, or Ranke. This conviction, first formally expressed in his famous presidential manifesto in 1933 to his fellow historians, "Written History as an Act of Faith," underlies all of his grapplings with the philosophy of history. The time had come, he felt, for historians to declare their emancipation from the intellectual formulas borrowed from natural science which had hobbled and distorted historical thinking. The historian could no longer go on believing "that the Newtonian trick will be turned some time," that the fullness of history can be captured in some deterministic scheme of "historical mechanics" in which events are illustrations of laws or can be arranged in "neat little chains of causation" linked by inexorable necessity. He had also to free himself from self-imposed subservience to biological analogies, giving up the illusion that societies are isolated organisms, subject to a deterministic morphology. The dream of a science of history, making possible calculable prediction of the future and summing up under law all past, present, and future occurrences, is the dream of omniscience.[5]

4. "That Noble Dream," *AHR, 41* (1935), 85. He was answering the criticism of Theodore Clarke Smith, "The Writing of American History in America, from 1884 to 1934," *AHR, 40* (1935), 447.

5. "Written History as an Act of Faith," *AHR, 39* (1934), 222-4.

The search for an overarching determinism is doomed to frustration, he felt, because all uniformities in human affairs are partial and local, mere islands of predictive certainty in an indeterminate sea. Man's knowledge falls far short of the omniscience required for a "celestial mechanics" of history as totality. Finite explanations cannot buy truth wholesale, and even the scientist, he argued, cannot explain the cosmos; he can only describe and predict. The shortcoming of all human efforts to explain is that they depend upon assumptions of relevancy which are controlled by the specific purposes of the explainer. In Beard's eyes the historian is placed in a specially precarious position: History, which he defined as the sum total of all human occurrences, must ever exceed the historian's grasp because not all facts have been recorded and many records have been lost. The historian cannot achieve scientific explanations because he can never be sure he has taken into account all the relevant facts, nor can the imponderables of history be expressed in the mathematical terms of measurement which give to science its precision and certainty. The historian's problems are not external phenomena having weight, extension, and velocity; they are mental tensions arising out of a conceptual frame of reference. Whenever the historian breaks the "seamless web" of history to pick out events and causes, he makes an act of will for some purpose related to his values and interests, which are, in turn, related to his political, economic, and social commitments. This frame of reference incorporates "things deemed necessary, things deemed possible, and things deemed desirable."[6] Fortunately, there are not, he felt, an

6. Ibid., p. 227. My sketch of Beard's theory is a composite based on his views as set forth in such other works as *A Charter for the Social Sciences in the Schools*, Report of the Commission on the Social Studies, American Historical Association (New York, Charles Scribner's Sons, 1932), Pt. I; *The Nature of the Social Sciences, in Relation to Objectives of Instruction*, ibid. (New York, Charles Scribner's Sons, 1934), Pt. VII; *The Open Door at Home; The Discussion of Human Affairs*, New York, Macmillan, 1936; "History and Social Science," *Saturday Review of Literature*, 12 (August 17, 1935), 9; and the articles cited above, notes 2–4.

infinite number of perspectives which historians can apply. Following Karl Mannheim, Beard noted five general types: (1) bureaucratic conservatism (which he had identified with the Ranke tradition); (2) historical conservatism (Edmund Burke's philosophy of the landed aristocracy); (3) bourgeois liberalism (middle-class parliamentarianism and free competition); (4) socialism (the "scientific history" of Karl Marx); and (5) fascism (the German and Italian revolutions based on myths). Within this limited relativity the historian can, by the scrupulous use of sources, achieve a measure of scientific exactness.[7]

Having urged upon historians the recognition of the relativity of history, Beard then desperately looked for a way out of the impasse relativism had created. There was, he felt, a need to cut the Gordian knot, a knot which Becker had so brilliantly tied in "Everyman His Own Historian." The apostle of relativity, confident that all historical conceptions are "merely relative to passing events, to transitory phases of ideas and interests," must, eventually, "be executed by his own logic."[8] Beard had shored up the crumbling foundations of historical knowledge by limiting the number of possible frames of reference; not every man could be his own historian. And Beard wanted even more stable ground upon which to take his stand. Faced with the totality of all times and circumstances and all relativities, the historian, he concluded, must come to a decision about the process of history as a whole. Whatever his frame of reference he must determine whether history is mere flux and chaos, or a natural process of cyclical recurrence, or, finally, progressive movement "on an upward gradient toward a more ideal order—as imagined by Condorcet, Adam Smith, Karl Marx, or Herbert Spencer."[9] Like Henry Adams, Beard charged the historian with

7. "Currents of Thought in Historiography," *AHR, 42* (1937), 481; *The Nature of the Social Sciences,* pp. 18–19.

8. "Written History as an Act of Faith," p. 225. Cf. his review of Becker's *The Heavenly City of the Eighteenth-century Philosophers,* in *AHR, 38,* (1933), 591.

9. "Written History as an Act of Faith," p. 226.

the responsibility of determining the direction of history as a process. But, unlike Adams, Beard saw no objective way of solving the problem. Any appeal to the facts will be inconclusive; the historian can only make "an act of faith." From this point of view the historian has to assume the risks of the statesman dealing with public affairs, "a statesman, without portfolio, to be sure, but with a kindred sense of responsibility."[10]

Beard was fully prepared to cross his own Rubicon. Looking backward as a historian and looking forward as a prophet with "a faith in the indomitable spirit of mankind," he committed himself to the position that history was moving forward to a dimly divined "collectivist democracy."[11] With this ringing defiance of the depression and vote of confidence in President Roosevelt, Beard, in the critical year of 1933, challenged his fellow historians to make their act of faith. Whatever his decision, the historian's influence and immortality would depend upon the accuracy of his divination of the future—"upon the verdict of history yet to come." The great historian, as he had first written in 1919 and still believed in 1946 when he made his last statement on the philosophy of history, reflects the "master current" of his age: "He endures only in so far as he succeeds in casting through the warp of the past the weft of the future—the future which he can behold only by prophetic discernment. It is given to but a few to walk with the gods in the dusk of ages."[12] It was Beard's ambition to join that select company.

Beard's philosophy of history as an act of faith has had both its defenders and its opponents among recent presidents of the American Historical Association.[13] The division of opinion reflects a pro-

10. *The Open Door at Home*, p. 138.
11. "Written History as an Act of Faith," p. 228.
12. "James Ford Rhodes," *New Republic, 21* (1919), 83.
13. See Conyers Read (who follows Beard in calling for an act of faith in the future), "The Social Responsibilities of the Historian," *AHR, 55* (1950), 284–5, and Samuel Eliot Morison (who reinvokes Ranke against Beard's "frame of reference"), "Faith of a Historian," *AHR, 56* (1951), 268.

found ambiguity in the theory itself. Like Becker, Beard was convincing in his attack on the historical positivism of scientific history, yet the arbitrariness of his final conclusions testifies to his own ambiguous relationship to the tradition he condemned. Having emancipated the historian from intellectual dependence on the formulas of science, he followed this declaration of independence with a manifesto of a new dependence. The justification of the historian's work lay outside himself in the verdict of future events. Having begun with an appeal for critical thinking, he ended with a demand for blind faith. The historian was to be a prophet whose predictions would be verified or rejected by future experience. In this way the scientific ideal of predictability curiously reappeared in the thinking of the liberator of historians from subservience to science.

If Beard frequently cited European thinkers in support of his position, he seems not to have realized they could often be quoted against him. Croce defined the historically disciplined mind as one that "distinguishes the hour for knowing and the hour for doing"; and he warned that the historian falsifies history by "turning it into a practical struggle" or by indulging that imagination of the future which is only the "mother of hopes and fears."[14] Just as the positivists had defended themselves by appealing to a misunderstood Ranke, so had Beard attacked them by appealing to a misunderstood Croce. The Italian philosopher, like Karl Heussi and Kurt Riezler, was concerned with the intellectual presuppositions of history as a mode of knowledge; Beard was anxious to define the vital faith necessary for the man of action. Even Karl Mannheim, who spoke in almost Beardian terms of the "necessity of wilfully choosing and . . . the need for an imperative (a utopia) to drive us onward," stressed the participation of the historian in the living context of social life not to discredit historical truth, but rather to emphasize that such involvement is "a presupposition of the understanding of

14. *History as the Story of Liberty*, trans. Sylvia Sprigge (New York, W. W. Norton, 1941), p. 286.

the inner nature of this living context." To describe objectivity as a disregard for qualitative elements and a complete restraint of the will is, he felt, to negate "the essential quality of the object." Participation in history makes insight and knowledge possible; it does not signify error or distortion. Beard's historical skepticism failed to acknowledge the force of Mannheim's point that skeptical relativism arises from recognition of the importance of participation in history only when the realization is linked "with the older static ideal of eternal, unperspectivistic truths independent of the subjective experience of the observer, and when it is judged by this alien ideal of absolute truth."[15]

It was precisely this alien ideal that still hovered before Beard's mind, darkening his vision with the specter of a vast totality, the historian's alleged "absolute," comprising all occurrences past, present, and becoming to the end of time. Only omniscience could grasp "the plan, law, philosophy, or sense of history."[16] The historian could not make this "break-through into the domain of absolute knowledge" to "grasp universal history in its internal fullness," and the impossibility tormented Beard, as if the historian could find truth only if he were God. For this reason he felt obliged to make an act of faith about the historical process as a whole. Thus

15. The above three references are from *Ideology and Utopia: An Introduction to the Sociology of Knowledge,* trans. Louis Wirth and Edward Shils (New York, 1949), pp. 234, 42, and 270, respectively. For a related criticism of Beard's understanding of European philosophers see Lloyd R. Sorenson, "Charles A. Beard and German Historiographical Thought," *Mississippi Valley Historical Review,* 42 (1955), 274–87.

16. Review of R. G. Collingwood, *The Idea of History,* in *AHR,* 52 (1947), 707. In a review of Henry Adams' *The Degradation of the Democratic Dogma* Beard expressed sympathy for Adams' search for a science of history which would predict the future, pointing out that the historian "may be like the poets, the men of science, and the theologians, a searcher for the key to things, for a law that will reduce history to order or explain the course of human events, just as the laws of natural science reveal the government of the material world." See "Henry Adams," *New Republic,* 22 (1920), 162.

he revived, in a new guise, Henry Adams' quest for a single spool on which to wind the threads of the past. From this point of view the entire course of events is assumed to have some plot, a web of meaning, over and above the specific empirical studies of the historian. But conceived of in this way the philosophy of history threatens both philosophy and history by being a hybrid mixture of each which destroys the integrity of the elements composing it. To see events as part of a vast cryptogram of time, which the historian can decipher only by an appeal beyond history to religious faith, to science, to metaphysics, or to some future ideal goal, "explains" history by the nonhistorical and creates an untenable dualism between events and their meaning. There are not two histories, a lesser one which the historian critically studies and a transcendental one which is comprehensible only by an extrahistorical flight of speculation. Philosophies of history constructed on this kind of antithesis tend to become allegories, mingling history with something else, whether theology, science, metaphysics, or politics. The late 19th century was filled with such speculative curiosities, which have survived, if at all, only because the polemical tendencies they express have made them fighting faiths for true believers.

Beard was frank in refusing to disguise his act of faith as a piece of higher knowledge, the fruit of some special insight or superior synthesis. He made his political commitment bluntly clear. Doing so, he exposed to view the basic difficulty of his theory: how can the historical past be comprehended in terms of a dimly discerned over-all goal, unless we are to look for illumination from a source which, being as yet undetermined, cannot provide any light? What the future holds is opaque to thought because only present action can determine what will happen. The predictions announced by the scientist do not refer to coming historical events; they merely declare the existence of natural regularities not yet directly observed. As Becker once remarked, the value of history is moral not scientific; it helps us to meet rather than to foretell the future. Only because the historian is a kind of prophet *after* the event, by virtue of a hindsight which can explain the event in terms of a knowledge of what came before it and after it that no participant in the event can have, is he capable of a historical objectivity which can rise above the passionate conflicts of the past.

Because Beard was unable to break the spell of the dream of an impossible omniscient knowledge, he drew skeptical conclusions from his recognition of the historian's inability to survey the past from some platform outside history. But the completely detached mind, insulated from all the pressures of living history in the world around it, would have no need for acquiring the orientation and perspective historical study can provide and consequently no desire to make that active exploration of documents which alone can bring the past to life. Furthermore, if the past bears vital relationships to the present, the historian who is not rooted in his own time can hardly expect to ask the kind of questions that will uncover them, and unless one asks the proper questions, history for the historian, like nature for the scientist, is a sphinx whose silence does not even provoke a riddle. In this sense the historian's present "frame of reference" does not distort the past; it brings it into focus.

For Beard, of course, a "frame of reference" is a fundamental limitation on the historian's power to explain the past because it incorporates within it his interests and values. No doubt the historian's values will make him especially alert to certain intellectual problems and insensitive to others; they will even give him better insight into some men and issues of the past than into others. Yet these limitations, if the historian is aware of them, need not make him despair of his craft. Beard, in fact, made an important contribution to the sophistication of American historians by urging them to become aware of their own values and to inform and illuminate them by knowledge and experience. Relativism becomes fatal to the integrity of history as a discipline only when the theory asserts with Beard that the historian's explanations are mere arbitrary intrusions into the "seamless web" of time, performed "for some purpose arising in human conceptions of values and interests."[17] How, he asked, can some events be isolated from preceding events and treated as causes apart from events that caused the causes? It seems plausible, he admitted, that German submarine warfare influenced Wilson to decide upon American intervention more than did the Kaiser's moustaches, but how can the historian ever be sure? For this reason Beard urged the historian to abandon the idea of "cause" altogether.

In this hypercriticism of historical knowledge he seems to have accepted the curious premise that nothing in particular can be explained until everything in general is explained. Yet all knowledge, in history no less than in science, depends upon the asking of restricted questions for which limited answers are sought. If everything is assumed to be relevant to everything else, there is no way to check any hypothesis by an appeal to specific evidence. Truth and error, under these conditions, can no longer be distinguished. Beard himself admitted that historians can obtain "accurate knowledge of historical facts, personalities, situations, and movements."[18] They can, for example, describe the situation, interests, ideas, choices, policy, and conclusions of the Founding Fathers at Philadelphia, for, after all, Beard claimed to have done just that. What historical scholarship cannot do, he stressed, is demonstrate that the action of the delegates at the Convention was "determined unequivocally by any set of circumstances or chain of previous events," nor can the historian derive from his inquiries "irrefragable rules for the determination of policy, present or future."[19] But why should these provisos make one a skeptic or a relativist? The margin of intellectual authority Beard was willing to grant historians seems quite sufficient to satisfy anyone not dazzled by the pretentious dream of a deterministic science of history. The limitations he emphasized were precisely those flouted by the scientific historians who yearned to discover a sort of historical mechanics which would yield laws for

17. *The Discussion of Human Affairs*, p. 79.
18. "Written History as an Act of Faith," p. 226.
19. *The Open Door at Home*, p. 26.

the guidance of policy-makers. Acknowledgment of his qualifications of the historian's power is no argument for skepticism unless the terms of the discussion are established by the scientific historians. Not only did their reach exceed their grasp; they pursued a false ideal. An explanation of a historical event as a mere link in a chain of events controlled by either a mechanical or an ideal necessity would rob history of any creativity, originality, or novelty. History as a pattern of human action would be explained away as the mere illustration of some nonhistorical system of forces. What is the dignity of the adjective "historical" when applied to an event if not its being an announcement that something new under the sun has happened? Just because of this unprecedented significance of history-making events, they cannot be simply deduced from antecedent circumstances; instead they illuminate their own past and force the retrospective eye to seek an understanding of them as a hitherto unrecognized fulfillment of a creative development.[20]

Beard knew that the pretentions of the scientific historians were doomed to frustration, but his own position was poignantly skeptical because it reflected his nostalgia for their hopes of achieving an all-embracing synthesis of the past. Both he and Becker tried to reorient American historical thought along humanistic lines. Yet in the end the underlying beliefs of the scientific historians with whom they quarreled arrested the progress of the revolt against scientific history. The thinking of Becker and Beard bears the marks of their struggle with the past. In this way, as if in revenge for the tricks historians may play on the dead, the dead hand of the past may still lie heavy on the innovating mind.

20. This point about the inapplicability of causal determinism to history is made by Hannah Arendt, "Understanding and Politics," *Partisan Review*, 20 (1953), 388.

PART TWO

The Revolt against Formalism

IN SPITE OF their intense concern for the philosophy of history, Becker and Beard were primarily historians, not philosophers. This distinction is an important one because the historian's ideas at the practical level of research and writing are of a different order from, and may even be better than, his ideas at the theoretical level of reflection. It is not surprising, accordingly, that with both men there are dissonant notes in their efforts to harmonize theory and practice. Becker's philosophical revolt against scientific history had its practical corollary in his emphasis on the inner, psychic dimension of history in contrast to the positivists' external and atomistic treatment of the past. This insight led him to stress the importance of individual character and the intellectual climate of opinion as historical factors. With Beard the theoretical attack on scientific history had its parallel in his determination to substitute an economic interpretation of history for "the germ theory of politics" and the mere chronicling of "what exactly happened." Yet insofar as both men aimed to provide more adequate explanations of historical changes, their practice of history conflicted, to this extent, with their philosophies of skeptical relativism.

The discrepancy is, in part, a reflection of a double purpose. When they wrote history they were not only challenging scientific historians; they were responding as well to Turner's plea to study "the vital forces" behind institutional and constitutional forms. In this respect they were a part of that broad movement which Morton G. White has aptly called "The Revolt against Formalism," trying to do for history what Dewey, Veblen, and Holmes were doing for philosophy, economics, and law.[1] The institutional school had grown up under the shadow of historical positivism. In its Darwin-

1. *Social Thought in America: The Revolt against Formalism* (New York, Viking, 1949), pp. 11–31.

ian phase it had developed "the germ theory" in directions that tended to provide pseudoscientific sanction for racist, imperialist, and conservative attitudes, as, for example, in the writings of Brooks Adams who was, like his brother Henry, a searcher for a deterministic, scientific philosophy of history. In more conventional writers Darwinism was the language of pious traditionalism: one historian, seeing the germs of our Constitution in "our Aryan ancestors," concluded that its "elemental forms were revealed to our fathers on the mounts of British history, as the patterns of the tabernacle were revealed to Moses on Sinai."[2] The inspiration of Ranke's example had also reinforced the predominant political and legal emphasis in American historical writing. One of his American students, Herbert Levi Osgood, who was to become a great intellectual pioneer in the study of colonial history, expressed this credo in 1898: "The political and constitutional side of the subject, it seems to me, should be given the first place, because it is only through law and political institutions that social forces become in the large sense operative."[3]

Although social and economic history had earlier American proponents in John B. McMaster and Edward Eggleston, their contributions had been marred either by mere cataloguing of events without any organizing principles or by sentimental antiquarianism.[4] Intellectual history was even more neglected. A few positivistically inclined historians, like John W. Draper and Andrew D. White, studied the history of ideas, but with the polemical purpose of establishing a science of history or of defending science in its warfare

2. James C. Welling, *Connecticut Federalism* (New York, New York Historical Society, 1890), p. 28.

3. "Study of American Colonial History," *American Historical Association, Annual Report* (1898), p. 68.

4. See Michael Kraus, *A History of American History* (New York, Farrar and Rinehart, 1937), pp. 393-4, and Charles Hirschfeld, "Edward Eggleston: Pioneer in Social History," *Historiography and Urbanization: Essays in American History in Honor of W. Stull Holt,* ed. Eric F. Goldman (Baltimore, Johns Hopkins University Press, 1941), p. 207.

with theology. Like Henry Adams they wrote intellectual history only in a European context. Not until the four volumes of Moses Coit Tyler's explorations of the literature of Colonial and Revolutionary America were published in the late 19th century did American thought find its historian, and when this single blaze of light subsided, the landscape was once again blanketed in darkness.[5] The positivistic description of events as externalized facts or impersonal laws contained an animus against the historical study of ideas.

In the 1920's a new generation of historians transformed the intellectual scene. The cooperatively written series on social history, *A History of American Life,* and Vernon L. Parrington's *Main Currents in American Thought,* linking literature with ideas and society, were characteristic landmarks of the new movement. Beard's powerful synthesis of American history—in terms of historical materialism and the idea of progress—and Becker's psychological insight into the interplay of character, ideas, and social forces represented significant contributions to this creative burst of the modern historical mind in America.

5. John Higham, "The Rise of American Intellectual History," *AHR, 56* (1951), 456–7.

CHAPTER FOUR

The Climate of Opinion and the Thin Red Line of Heroes

B Y CONVENTIONAL STANDARDS Becker's historical writings have two shortcomings: brevity and only a modest amount of original research. He had no desire to impress his readers by his scope or his labor; he had quite other purposes and achieved a different distinction. All of his writing, which was centered around the period of the 18th century, bears the marks of originality in conception, subtlety in interpretation, and graciousness in style. It was characteristic of the man to apply these talents even in a high-school text on modern history and in an account of Benjamin Franklin for an encyclopedia, both efforts being widely recognized as outstanding examples of a genre seldom rising above the commonplace. With Becker these gifts of mind were not merely ornamental virtues; they were the delicate instruments by which he gave vivid life to his vision of history. It is the lesson of his work that the historian must take account of the role of individual character, of the intellectual presuppositions of an age, and of the importance of narrative technique. The success of his revolt against both scientific history and the formalism of the institutional school of political and constitutional history is measured by these three contributions.

In Becker's eyes the dogmas of an earlier generation of historians had led them to produce a narrative of events "so externalized, so reduced to commonplace matter of fact, so purged of any sense of life, of the presence of human passions," that it "might have occurred at any time and in any place, given a sufficient number of persons to operate the events."[1] He felt that it was useless to record what men did without asking why they had done it. Apart from an understanding of the men who made and suffered events, the historian could not even determine "what really happened," and this understanding required a more profound analysis of individual motivation and the genesis of social ideas than American historians had yet made. In these terms Becker charted his course as a historian.

His recognition of the significance of the individual in history was demonstrated by the courses he taught at Cornell on representative Americans and Europeans and in a brilliant series of essays on such figures as Franklin, Jefferson, Diderot, Madame Roland, Sam Adams, Thomas Hutchinson, and many others. These studies were, indirectly, a salutary rebuke to the scientific historians who, by reducing the individual to "a mere chance deposit on the surface of the world, and the odd chance and recalcitrant event to a negligible exception to the rule,"[2] distorted history into impersonal forces and abstract laws. The historian, he felt, is necessarily a man with an eye for the concrete and the unique. He has to study the purposes of men, knowing that the motives which inspire human conduct are many and variously combined, never exerting quite the same pressure in any two situations. For this reason Becker was wary of any attempt "to pack the human spirit" in the "syllogistic handbag"[3] of economic determinism. His essay "John Jay and Peter Van Schaack" specifically dramatized the failure of any such abstract theory of human conduct as a principle of historical explanation. Both Jay and Van Schaack were attached to America, both were opposed to British measures of control over the colonies, both were

1. "Harnessing History," *New Republic, 22* (1920), 322.
2. Becker, *Cornell University: Founders and the Founding* (Ithaca, Cornell University Press, 1943), p. 41. Further evidence of his concern for the individual in history is his "Memorandum Concerning a Department of Biography," July 8, 1944, Becker Papers.
3. "Idealistic Forces in American History," *Dial, 56* (1914), 141.

successful lawyers and substantial men of property, both were political conservatives—yet in 1778 Jay became a member of the committee that signed the decree of exile against his friend Van Schaack
as a traitor to his country. If both men had sided with America or
both with Britain, or even if their positions had been reversed, the
idea of economic self-interest would still be applied by the determinist with "equal complacence" to "explain" their conduct. But
a theory claiming to cover all possibilities cannot satisfactorily account for any one of them. By explaining too much it forfeits its
verifiability and usefulness. To solve the problem the historian,
seeking for causes, must penetrate instead to those "more subtle and
impalpable influences"[4] which underlie motive and conduct.

Becker's probings beneath the level of deliberate and self-conscious purpose were not conducted in the facile style of the New
History, as defended by Harry Elmer Barnes, who "explained"
Jefferson's outlook, program, and party as "an elaborate disguise
and secondary rationalization" due to "the recoil of the pallid youth
of Shadwell from his gigantic and formidable father."[5] Becker did
not have the partisan animus of the "de-bunker" with his dogmatic
assurance that he knows the bad "real reasons" beneath the apparent
"good reasons." For Becker the division between Jay and Van
Schaack was produced by moral values as well as by temperament
and circumstance. The sanguine and sociable Jay, more inclined to
stress the evils of submission to Great Britain and morally convinced
that the time had come to declare one's allegiance, signed the Articles of Association out of a sense of duty to his colleagues in Congress. The aloof and pessimistic Van Schaack, temperamentally
more sensitive to the evils of war and isolated from Congress with
his sick and grieving family at Kinderhook, refused, for his part, to
surrender his moral right to decide for himself alone whether it was

4. *Everyman His Own Historian* (New York, Appleton Century Crofts,
1935), p. 287.
5. *The New History and the Social Studies* (New York, Century, 1925),
pp. 24–5.

his duty to join in the measures advocated by the patriots. In Becker's account the key to the action of the two men is not some kernel which can be extracted from the husk of their situation; it is instead a continual, organic interplay of character, circumstance, and events.

Similarly, he explored the "hidden springs of conduct" in Madame Roland not to show her up as a bogus revolutionary but to solve a problem posed by the ambiguity of the documents themselves: a puzzling discrepancy between her memoirs and her letters. In her letters she revealed herself to be a woman who accepted the pre-Revolutionary regime as a matter of course, who had only a perfunctory interest in politics, and who was dissatisfied with the world for the conventional reason that she was socially ambitious for herself and husband. Yet in her memoirs, written in prison under the shadow of the guillotine, she stands forth as "a pure republican soul, hating kings, despising *ces pitoyables anoblis,* instinctively preparing herself, perhaps even without knowing it, for her destiny during that Revolution which she could not foresee."[6] For the Ranke-inspired positivists the memoirs would simply be regarded as an untrustworthy source; for the psychological "debunkers" they would be mere idealistic rationalizations to protect her from the sordid reality of her cell. What Becker showed was that she shaped her memoirs by idealizing them to ready herself for her imminent death. She saw her career as a long mission leading to martyrdom for human liberty and appealed to posterity for her justification. This gesture was more than a compensatory one because both the memoirs and the letters, despite their inconsistencies, reveal her capacity for self-dramatization, her need to find adequate scope for her energies and intelligence, and her ambitions for something less commonplace than her actual life. These qualities were nonetheless real for being frustrated, nor was her ideal image of herself an

6. "The Memoirs and the Letters of Madame Roland," in *Everyman His Own Historian,* pp. 308–9.

illusion. He ventured to think, in fact, that her ideal character became at last the real Madame Roland, so that by the time she went in her tumbril to the guillotine she had become a heroic *philosophe*, faithful to the aspirations of her age as mirrored in her memoirs.

In his concern for individual character in history Becker's writings are quite unorthodox from the point of view of the New History, with its theoretical commitment to the study of social forces as an antidote to romantic hero worship and melodramatic sensationalism. Historians of this school condemned their colleagues for sitting down to tell sad tales of the death of kings when they might be up and doing, busily chronicling the small beer of the common man. But Becker realized that individuals are important precisely because they are the points of intersection, the loci of conflicts of great social forces. In them the process of history comes alive. This process, he knew, is not transcendental, "something in the void working over the heads of men, rough hewing them to its own ends." He had learned from his teacher Turner that it is "something that emerges from the thought and action of men, something incidental to what people do for their own ends."[7]

When Becker probed the characters of John Jay and Peter Van Schaack, he was doing something more than explaining individual behavior; he was highlighting the narrow line that separated Tories from Patriots. In shading this line so delicately he rubbed out the crude black-and-white portrait of the issue as a conflict between sheep and goats. His *Beginnings of the American People* and *The Eve of the Revolution* performed a similar service on a broader scale. He focused the Revolution in the dramatic antagonism of Sam Adams, leader of the Sons of Liberty, and Thomas Hutchinson, royal governor of Massachusetts. In making a personal tragedy out of Hutchinson's exile from the country he loved, because of Adams' accusations that the governor's letters to an English friend were treasonable, Becker showed how the exasperation of the two men

7. "Frederick Jackson Turner," ibid., p. 214.

with each other was something more than a merely personal hostility. In their conflict was dramatized the growing division between men who clung to legal rights and men who affirmed "natural rights," between those who opposed Parliament's measures without denying its ultimate authority and those who saw the harsh mien of despotism in any control over colonial affairs. When the middle ground finally crumbled away, Adams and Hutchinson embodied the only alternatives left to the colonists, compelled to make the choice that would divide Rebels from Loyalists: they must recognize the authority of agitators proclaiming the rights of the people at home as well as the right of colonial home rule or accept the authority of an imperial power.[8]

If the scientific historians had failed to take account of the importance of individuals because of a devotion to impersonal laws and forces, the idolization of Ranke as the apostle of literal-mindedness prevented them from asking the kind of questions Becker was particularly interested in raising. The conception of history as the external story of "what actually happened" made it difficult, if not impossible, to conceive of intellectual history. Yet the historian is blinded if he thinks of history as made up only of events as tangible as the Boston Tea Party or the storming of the Bastille. "The silent change which took place in people's ideas about nature and her laws," Becker pointed out, "is one of the most important events in modern history—far more important than the wars and battles that made much more noise at the time; for without this change modern science, and the mastery of material forces which depends on science would have been impossible."[9] Similarly, historians under the influence of Ranke, as interpreted by American positivists, missed the

8. *Beginnings of the American People,* Riverside History of the United States, ed. William E. Dodd, *1* (Boston, Houghton Mifflin, 1915), pp. 244–5; *The Eve of the Revolution,* The Chronicles of America, ed. Allen Johnson, *11* (New Haven, Yale University Press, 1918), pp. 158–99.

9. Becker, *Modern History: The Rise of a Democratic, Scientific, and Industrialized Civilization* (rev. ed. New York, Silver Burdett, 1941), p. 176.

significance of the mental atmosphere of documents they scanned merely to find a report on what happened. Ardently interested in facts, they failed, for example, "to note a fact that is writ large in the most authentic documents: the fact that the thought of posterity was apt to elicit from eighteenth-century Philosophers . . . a highly emotional, an essentially religious response."[10]

To explore intellectual history, Becker felt, required a more subtle approach than the search for "influences," as if it were merely a question of finding out from what book Jefferson got his ideas for the Declaration of Independence. It was necessary rather to discover the intellectual and social situation which made it possible for Jefferson and his colleagues to believe that the right of revolution and the philosophy of natural rights, contained within the Declaration, were only "the common sense of the matter." In mock lament, poking fun at the cult of "influences," Becker complained that because David Hume had locked up in his desk his *Dialogues Concerning Natural Religion,* instead of publishing them, the historian was unhappily prevented from citing them as the cause of the trend of 18th-century speculation away from metaphysics to history, morality, and politics. "A history lost and all for the want of a petty date!"[11] But, as Becker pointed out, if the book had been an "influence," it would have been so only because the minds of its readers were already prepared to accept its message. The important question, therefore, is not whom did the book influence but why was it written in the first place. To answer it the historian would have to investigate the climate of opinion in which the book had been written.

For Becker, analyzing the "climate of opinion" (a phrase borrowed from the philosopher Whitehead) was a method of achieving order and synthesis by dealing with the various activities of a period "as illustrating, or as related to, certain mental or psychic

10. *The Heavenly City of the Eighteenth-century Philosophers,* p. 142.
11. Ibid., p. 72.

characteristics common to the social group."[12] It was a principle he had practiced in one of his earliest essays, a study of Kansas as a state of mind, a transplantation of Puritanism and Americanism to frontier conditions; and he brought it to a fine fruition in his brilliant treatment of the French and American Enlightenment in *The Heavenly City of the Eighteenth-century Philosophers* and *The Declaration of Independence*. The clue to any age, he felt, can be found in the concepts which serve as fundamental, unquestioned postulates of its outlook. These ideas, appearing unobtrusively and pervasively, are seldom analyzed, because they are the basis on which everything else is analyzed by the people that use them. Thus in the 18th century, amid all the clash of contrary opinion, "nature" and "natural law" were the terms which provided common ground for all the controversialists. The deist Voltaire, the atheist Holbach, and the Christian Bishop Butler, despite their differences, made common appeal to the authority of the book of nature and the workings of natural law. The tradition was an old one, but the 18th century gave it a new meaning. Whereas the thinker of the Middle Ages concluded that "nature *must* be rational because God *is* eternal reason," the man of the Enlightenment, like Hume's character, Cleanthes, in his *Dialogues,* concluded that "God *must* be an engineer because nature *is* a machine."[13] This reversal of premises is the clue, the secret key, that unlocks the mind of the Enlightenment.

Becker realized that the ideas which form a climate of opinion are not in fixed solution; they suffer tensions and breed conflicts. It was for this reason that Hume had locked his *Dialogues* in his desk and that Diderot had mysteriously ceased publishing his writing after 1765. The philosophers wanted to believe that since man was shaped by a nature which God had created, it was possible for men, by the use of their natural faculties, to bring their institutions into

12. "Some Aspects of the Influence of Social Problems and Ideas upon the Study and Writing of History," *Publications of the American Sociological Society,* 7 (1913), 112.

13. *The Heavenly City,* p. 56.

harmony with the natural order of things. It was this doctrine which provided them with a basis for criticizing the evils of the *ancien régime*. Yet if man really was a product of nature, all that he did and thought must also be natural and in harmony with the laws of nature and of nature's God. From this point of view even the *ancien régime,* with all its terrors and evils of despotism and superstition, was a necessary part of the natural order of things. The metaphysics of the philosophers had led them to a materialism which could not support either man's free will or the goodness of God. To read Hume's *Dialogues* in this light is, Becker remarked, to experience a feeling of apprehension, as if, "at high noon of the Enlightenment, at the hour of the siesta when everything seems so quiet and secure all about, one were suddenly aware of a short, sharp slipping of the foundations, a faint far-off tremor running underneath the solid ground of common sense."[14] To find support for their crusade against kings, nobles, and clergy the *philosophes* had to abandon metaphysical speculation and try instead to construct a new vision of the past and the future to buttress their "Heavenly City."

For Becker "the specious present," the unity in consciousness of the sense of the past and the vision of the future, was a concept applicable to the mind of an age, or its climate of opinion. Thus he showed how the historians of the 18th century, like Gibbon and Voltaire, created an image of the past which made the writing of history a weapon in the warfare against tyranny and superstition. History was a matter of teaching morality and philosophy by example. The times to be condemned were those "Dark Ages" when the Christian Church held sway. The *quatre âges heureux,* as Voltaire called them, were the golden days of Pericles and Augustus, the Renaissance, and, of course, the enlightened 18th century. As for the future, the philosophers revised the Christian story, without losing its drama or its happy ending, by forecasting the perfectibility of man and seeking their justification in the memories of a grateful

14. Ibid., pp. 68–9.

posterity, which was for Madame Roland, as it was for Diderot, what "the other world" had been for the medieval mind.

With a similar sensitivity to the mentality behind documents, challenging the exercise of the historical imagination, Becker explored the American Enlightenment by an analysis of the Declaration of Independence and the hidden meaning implicit in its argument and language. Only one chapter in *The Declaration of Independence* could have given comfort to the worshipers of fact. There he painstakingly reconstructed the changes in the draftings of the document, which he traced by an intricate comparison of its various copies. This kind of historical criticism, which Ranke's example had taught many historians, Becker practiced well, but his real concern was to reveal the climate of opinion which the Declaration expressed and presupposed in its appeal to "self-evident" truths and "the laws of Nature and of Nature's God."

Studied as a mere report, the document is a list of grievances charged against the king, and by comparing it with the actual measures of imperial policy the historian is likely to conclude only that the king was less vicious and less irresponsible than the rebels made him out to be. Through Becker's eyes, however, the reader sees that the Declaration justifies revolution by an appeal to the philosophy of natural rights and implicitly asserts the colonists' theory of the British Empire as a commonwealth of virtually autonomous nations. By 1776, hammered out under the pressure of the ten-year dispute with the mother country, this climate of opinion appeared to the colonists as "the commonsense of the matter." Though in actuality Parliament, and not the king, had been the oppressor, the colonists attacked the king because they had come to believe that Parliament had no authority in the Empire. They had paid their respects to the king, as its nominal head, to whom they owed a sentimental allegiance, but since he had acted badly, the Declaration implied, they no longer owed him anything. The king, in fact, they said, had forfeited all claim to loyalty by outrageously neglecting his duties to the colonies.[15] Illuminated by Becker's imaginative understanding, what might otherwise seem to be only a formal announcement of independence or an exaggerated petition of grievances takes on a profound historical meaning.

In the age of scientific history, with its ideal of the bare statement of fact in bald language, style was unimportant; but for Becker, who himself commanded a style of rare grace, the language of the Declaration was itself a significant piece of evidence. Jefferson's "felicity of expression" was not merely ornamental, it was a window opening up a view of the man and his climate of opinion. This felicity, with its sonorous rhythm and "glittering generalities," expressed the confidence in human nature, the sense of high purpose, even the complacency and dogmatism, so characteristic of the *philosophes:* "Not without reason was Jefferson most at home in Paris. By the qualities of his mind and temperament he really belonged to the philosophical school, to the Encyclopaedists, those generous souls who loved mankind by virtue of not knowing too much about men, who worshipped reason with unreasoning faith, who made a religion of Nature while cultivating a studied aversion for 'enthusiasm,' and strong religious emotion."[16]

Becker's talent for seeing documents not as mere reports of what happened but as revelations of the mind that made them inevitably led him to at least partial abandonment of the narrative, chronological method of conventional historical writing. The danger of the story-telling approach is, of course, that it assumes that events need only to be related to be understood, instead of being problems that provoke the exercise of the historical imagination. Yet, as Becker clearly realized, history is a moving process, and to describe an evolution one must narrate the movement of events. The analysis of social forces or climates of opinion requires the method of generalized description; an account of their genesis and develop-

15. *The Declaration of Independence: A Study in the History of Political Ideas* (New York, Knopf, 1942), pp. 3–23, 80–134.
16. Ibid., p. 219.

ment demands a narration of the forward march of events: "The generalization, being timeless, will not move forward; and so the harassed historian, compelled to get on with the story, must return in some fashion to the individual, the concrete event, the 'thin red line of heroes.' Employing these two methods, the humane historian will do his best to prevent them from beating each other to death within the covers of his book."[17]

Becker's solutions to this problem were characteristically inventive and appropriate to his humanistic vision of history. His earliest and most powerful ambition was to be a writer, and it was, perhaps, only a matter of circumstance that he found an outlet for it in being a teacher and historian. It was no accident, however, that his favorite novelist was Henry James, who had a similar feeling for the nuances of motive and the organic relation between character and plot, or that he was fascinated by James Joyce, whose experiments with the stream of consciousness genre also reflected an interest in "the specious present."[18] It is not surprising, therefore, that Becker used the methods of a novelist to dramatize his account of the American Revolution in two studies, a book and an essay, which are already on their way to becoming modern classics of historical interpretation: *The Eve of the Revolution* and "The Spirit of '76."

In his preface to the book Becker declared that his primary concern was to tell how men had thought and felt about what they had done. To communicate "the quality of the thought and feeling of those days" and to enable the reader "to enter into such states of mind and feeling" he employed methods which could not be judged by "a mere verification of references."[19] The main departure from

17. "Frederick Jackson Turner," in *Everyman His Own Historian*, pp. 229–30.

18. Charlotte Watkins Smith, *Carl Becker: On History and the Climate of Opinion* (Ithaca, 1956), pp. 126–7. I learned of Becker's interest in Joyce's *Ulysses* from a former student of his, James C. Malin of the University of Kansas.

19. *The Eve of the Revolution*, pp. vii–viii.

conventional narration was his use of fictional paraphrases of what somebody might have said, the technique generally being applied to representative members of important social, political, and economic groups. Typically, these dramatizations of attitudes were indirectly paraphrased, rather than being direct quotations put in the mouth of a specific individual: "Many of them [West Indian sugar planters] were rich men no doubt; but sugar planting, they would assure you in confidence, was not what it had been; and if they were well off after a fashion, they might have been much better off but for the shameless frauds which for thirty years had made a dead letter of the Molasses Act of 1733."[20] In these devices Becker was never giving free reign to his fancy. They were always based on actual letters, diaries, state papers, or other documents, for he commanded a wide and deep knowledge of the sources for the period, which he had first intensively studied in his doctor's thesis. To increase further the illusion of direct participation in the events of the time he also used the strategy of moving the camera eye of the historian into a close-up perspective of such historically significant individuals as Benjamin Franklin, Samuel Adams, and Thomas Hutchinson. Throughout the book Becker kept his unconventional techniques from dominating him. If, as narrator and commentator, he sometimes slightly withdrew for the sake of the drama, he always returned to the foreground for the sake of historical judgment, making clear his theme that the colonists "fashioned their minds as well as their houses on good English models" and so guarded their legislative independence with jealous care, for a "hypersensitiveness in matters of taxation they knew to be the virtue of men standing for liberties which Englishmen had once won and might lose before they were well aware."[21]

The modest urbanity of his style, a deliberate reaction against

20. Ibid., p. 26. Cf. pp. 36, 48, 84, 103–4. His doctor's thesis was "The History of Political Parties in the Province of New York, 1760–1776," *Bulletin of the University of Wisconsin, History Series*, 2 (April 1909), 1–320.
21. *The Eve of the Revolution*, pp. 60–1.

the florid rhetoric of those historians who spoke in the majestic and measured tones they considered suitable to "the stately march of great events," was an appropriate instrument for the exposition of his view of the Revolution. Epic grandeur, however fitting for an account of "the Trojan War or the Fall of Lucifer,"[22] was out of place in depicting the conservative colonials moving, almost against their better judgment, toward a final separation from their mother country so lamentably fallen upon evil days from the heights of her glorious past. Through Becker's eyes we see how the conflict over home rule within the Empire, aggravated by the struggle over whether radicals or conservatives should rule at home, gradually led the colonists, hopeful that a show of unity might bring last-minute concessions from Parliament, to take steps they could no longer retrace: "In this gingerly way did the deputies lift the curtain and peer down the road to revolution."[23] Thus by 1776 they were ripe for Tom Paine's successful effort to convince them that independence was an act they freely willed, instead of being an event in which they had become entangled by a web of circumstance.

In "The Spirit of '76" Becker told the same story on a much smaller scale and by even more unconventional techniques. His essay was cast in the form of an edited fragment of a diary (quite imaginary) supposedly written by Jeremiah Wynkoop (also imaginary) in 1792 as a memoir of the years from 1763 to 1776. Wynkoop's relation to his father-in-law, a Dutch landowner of great wealth who finally becomes a Tory, and Wynkoop's own development into a reluctant rebel sum up in brilliant condensation Becker's other narratives of the Revolution. Using his familiar concept of the "specious present," he dramatized the break-up of his hero's "little world of opinion and conduct, held together by recollection of the past and hope for the future," when he discovers that Britain has declared the colonists to be in rebellion and his father-in-law

22. "Labelling the Historians," in *Everyman His Own Historian*, p. 139.
23. *The Eve of the Revolution*, p. 214.

has broken off relations with him. Paine's *Common Sense* and the support of Wynkoop's friends finally reassure him that Britain is no longer worthy of loyalty, thus repairing "the illusions by which he lived, reconciling himself to the inevitable step."[24] Just as Becker had used the "climate of opinion" and the "specious present," ideas first formulated in connection with his relativism, to analyze the Heavenly City of the 18th-century philosophers, so here he brought them into service again to explore the making of the revolutionary mind in America.

Becker's literary imagination, working hand in hand with his capacity for an empathic understanding of the past, enabled him to put into practice his belief that the historian must treat explanatory causes as "implicit in the events themselves and not to be identified with certain particular events separated out of the complex and taken as the sole or primary activating agencies."[25] To abstract some events as causes, shaping history from the outside, arbitrarily ruptures the historical process unless the historian can make experiments which eliminate variables and discover constants. But how can he experiment on a past which no longer exists? Causal judgment, furthermore, in the scientific sense presupposes law, regularity, and recurrence, yet the historian studies the American Revolution, for example, not primarily as an instance of a general category of social upheaval but as a unique crisis in the development of a particular society. Becker's practice of history implied that the historian's ideal of explanation is to tell his story with such an organic coherence of climate of opinion, individual or group purposes, and concrete circumstances that any question of an outside explanation of his narrative is superfluous. Like the novelist in this respect, he wants

24. "The Spirit of '76," in *Everyman His Own Historian*, pp. 74, 76.
25. "The Function of the Social Sciences," *Science and Man*, ed. Ruth Nanda Anshen (New York, Harcourt, Brace, 1942), p. 264. Thus he wrote to Louis Gottschalk that causes, for the historian, "are not on the scientific level or the philosophical level, but on the practical level of everyday life." Letter, Sept. 3, 1944, Becker Papers.

his plot and his characters to explain each other by the intelligibility of their relations as understood in human, purposive terms, so that to ask him to explain his story after he has told it is to accuse him of a failure to tell it properly. "History," as Becker noted, "tells us *what,* but if we ask her *why,* she can answer only by giving us more of the *what.*"[26]

No student of Becker's historical writing can help being struck by the talent it displays for an imaginative understanding of the past. Yet, just as clearly, his relativism creates the impression that the historian can never escape the blinders of his own "specious present" and "climate of opinion," which, responding to the dominant social forces of the day, generate those hopes and fears that prompt him to color the past into a useful image, giving him peace of mind in a stormy present. Becker's theory denies the possibility of achieving what his books have been justly praised for doing: recreating the life of a past period animated by a different spirit from the one prevailing in the historian's own time. Either his philosophy or his history must be fallacious.

From the relativistic point of view a critic might say that Becker's interpretations of the Enlightenment and the American Revolution were themselves tinged with the skeptical, disenchanted mood that pervaded so much of American intellectual life after the end of the first World War. Becker even implied just such a connection when he wrote, in bitterness against the war and the peace, that *The Eve of the Revolution* mirrored his belief in the impotence of men, whose principles are at the mercy of their hidden impulses, to understand or control the events they must face.[27] Yet if the historian can apply relativism to Becker himself, hoisting him with his own petard, in doing so the historian believes that he is stating a historical truth

---

26. *Modern History,* p. 497. Michael Oakeshott presents a cogent argument for a coherence-view of historical causation in *Experience and Its Modes* (Cambridge, Cambridge University Press, 1933), pp. 127–43.

27. Phil L. Snyder, "Carl L. Becker and the Great War: A Crisis for a Humane Intelligence," *Western Political Quarterly, 9* (March 1956), 6.

and not merely reflecting the transient sentiment of his day. A judgment charging bias due to relativity must always be comparative, implying a possible standard of greater objectivity, or the accusation becomes meaningless. When he found it in the thought of the 18th century, Becker clearly realized that a consistent relativism is a form of intellectual suicide. In one of his notes, made while studying the Enlightenment, he wrote: "Doctrine of Relativity if logically applied, if carried out completely goes too far and it undermines thought itself and truth and knowledge . . . Relativity becomes a convenient weapon for destructive criticism, but useless for constructing a system of knowledge."[28] It is ironical that the fallacy he recognized as a historian he committed as a philosopher.

If the tone and temper of Becker's writing, partially due to his cultural environment, sometimes gave a false air of donnish urbanity and slight condescension to his treatment of events, the substance of his work has been nevertheless widely recognized as making an important contribution to our objective understanding of the historical past. If his concepts of the "climate of opinion" and the "specious present" were better tools for historical analysis of the past than they were for philosophical definition of historical knowledge, it was largely because as a historian he was dealing with thought clearly implicated in a pragmatic context of social action. It is significant that in *The Heavenly City of the Eighteenth-century Philosophers* he developed his pragmatic relativism alongside his exposition of the mind of the Enlightenment. Though Voltaire, Hume, and Gibbon were not men of action like Jefferson, "Wynkoop," and the patriots of '76, they too treated the past in a pragmatic spirit. Often criticized for their antihistorical tendencies, the men of the Enlightenment used the past as a weapon in the crusade for progress against the evils of kings, priests, and nobles. These historians thus served as an ideal illustration of Becker's philosophy of history. His pragmatic relativism simply arrested the idea of his-

28. "Miscellaneous," Notes, drawer 15, Becker Papers.

tory at the stage of its immature development in the age of the Enlightenment. As Becker was fully aware, in reading Gibbon's famous
history of Rome we do not enter the Middle Ages or relive a span
of past experience; we see rather from the perspective of the "enlightened" 18th century "a thousand years filled with dim shapes of
men moving blindly, performing strangely, in an unreal shadowy
world."[29]

Yet by his very awareness of the limitations of the 18th-century
historians, his sense of their antihistorical leanings, and his ability
to define their outlook with a detachment from their premises, he
necessarily implied and practiced a superior standard of historical
interpretation—a standard which his philosophy not only failed to
defend but tended to deny. D. H. Lawrence, the novelist, once said
that we should trust the artist's story and not his opinions. We are
with Becker richly compensated for the weaknesses of his philosophy
by the profound artistry of his story. "As for you," Charles Beard
wrote Becker, "I have heard on good authority that you are no
Historian; nothing except a Man of Letters. It makes me jealous."[30]

29. *The Heavenly City*, p. 117.
30. Letter, Sept. 26 [no year], Becker Papers.

CHAPTER FIVE

Civilization and the Market Place

I ONLY want you to know that anything from your pen is always an event for me,"[1] Carl Becker, late in his life, wrote to Charles Beard. Though never an economic determinist, Becker, as an admiring student of Turner, who had urged historians to uncover the social and economic life shaping formal institutions, responded sympathetically to Beard's economic interpretation of history, noting that he had modernized "the ancient lady Clio, famous for her spotless flowing robes," into an up-to-date "flapper."[2] Beard wanted to do for Clio what he felt Roscoe Pound had done for "Miss Absolute Justice" and V. L. Parrington had done for "Miss Beautiful Letters": to yank her down from "her cold marble throne," hand her an apron, and "put her to work in a mundane place where she could learn about lives of men and women, loving and hating, acquiring and spending, hoping and fearing."[3] Beard did not, of course, invent the economic interpretation of history, nor was he the first to apply it to the American past, but no American historian had ever before used it with as much depth and breadth or with so powerful an influence. When the *New Republic* ran a symposium in 1938 on "Books That Changed Our Minds," no writer was cited by other intellectuals more often than Beard, and the wide acceptance of his views on the making of the Constitution and the coming of the Civil War in the great majority of college

1. Letter, May 10, 1943, Becker Papers.
2. Becker, "Fresh Air in American History," *Nation, 124* (1927), 560.
3. Beard, "Fresh Air in American Letters," ibid.

textbooks on American history made his impress vivid to thousands of students.[4]

There is a sharp spice of irony in Beard's acceptance of economic determinism as the natural fulfillment of the antiformalist revolt. He felt that Turner had violated his own antiformalist principles by becoming entangled in the abstract simplicities of the frontier hypothesis. "I wonder," Beard wrote Becker, "whether the weary world can ever get enthused again over some simple theory of history. It was grand to be alive in Queen Victoria's hopeful age when Darwins were hidden in every clump of academic bushes."[5] Yet in its own day Beard's historical writing once again aroused a weary world, this time to enthusiasm over the simple theory of economic determinism, which he linked to the hopeful promise of the idea of progress. Beard's revolt against scientific history, since it led him to attack determinism, eventually forced him to revise his economic interpretation of history; but he never quite lost his conviction of the pragmatic utility of searching for final explanations in the economic order. In this respect Beard the historian was faithful, after his fashion, to Beard the philosopher. As he modified his economic approach, however, in the light of his criticism of scientific history, his practice tended more and more to conform to his philosophical conviction that written history was an act of faith in progress "on an upward gradient toward a more ideal order." With his speculative ambition to encompass the course of events, envisaged as a movement toward some grand goal, by a sweeping theory, Beard was a Victorian, speaking in the tone and manner of a modern rebel.

4. *Books That Changed Our Minds: A Symposium,* ed. Malcolm Cowley and Bernard Smith (New York, Kelmscott, 1939), p. 19; Maurice Blinkoff, *The Influence of Charles A. Beard upon American Historiography,* University of Buffalo Studies, 12, Monographs in History, No. 4 (1936), 28, 51, 69.

5. Letter, Feb. 4 [no year], Becker Papers. Probably should be dated 1939, since it concerns Beard's "The Frontier in American History," *New Republic,* 97 (1939), 359–62.

Beard's father—a farmer, building contractor, and bank president —had been, in his son's words, "a copper-riveted, rock-ribbed, Mark Hanna, true-blue Republican,"[6] but there had been an appealing vein of unorthodoxy in an earlier ancestor upon which the future historian could draw for sustenance. In Beard's sturdy independence of mind, which on different occasions irritated liberals and conservatives alike, there is, perhaps, a touch of his grandfather, a rebel Quaker who ran a one-man church and boasted a library of several hundred volumes of comparative religion. Beard himself attended a Quaker academy until he was eighteen, and it is no accident that as a mature historian he celebrated the early American Quaker John Woolman as the spiritual father of American radicals who attacked the passion for acquisition as the root of evil.[7] Through his editorial work on the Knightstown *Banner,* purchased by his father, and later as a reporter for the Henry County *Republican,* the young Beard became aware of a world in which new forces contended against the orthodoxy of his father. As a student at DePauw University in his home-state of Indiana, he had debated the income tax proposal and labor's right to organize; and his teacher, Colonel James R. Weaver, had introduced him to the exciting intellectual systems of Karl Marx, Ruskin, and other social theorists of the Industrial Revolution. In the summer of 1896 in Chicago he acquired a first-hand acquaintance with the social settlement work at Hull House, contemporary labor problems, and the Populist agrarian protest as voiced in memorable rhetoric by William Jennings Bryan at the Democratic National Convention. When Beard went to England as a graduate student, he committed himself enthusiastically to the forces challenging the old order by joining with a Kansan socialist, Walter Vrooman, in 1899 to found Ruskin Hall,

6. *Current Biography* (1941), p. 52.
7. Charles A. and Mary R. Beard, *The Rise of American Civilization,* Vol. *1* of the series of the same title (rev. college ed. New York, Macmillan, 1934), p. 161.

the first laboring man's college at Oxford.[8] Through the "black country" of England's industrial towns with their "dark, Satanic mills" Beard spread the gospel of workers' education: "Let us hope that the new century will witness the triumph of the Co-operative ideal, and that humanity will have freed itself from the injustice, ignorance, and folly which to-day allow the few to live upon the toil of the many."[9]

In his first book, *The Industrial Revolution*, written in 1901 to further the cause of workers' education, he found "the central theme of history" in man's victory over "priestcraft, feudal tyrants, and warring elements." Man's future lay in his increasing assertion of "his right and power to determine his own religion and politics, and corporately to control every form of his material environment."[10] Convinced that scientists and inventors, like James Watt, the hero of his book, had demonstrated that "by attention, observation, and experiment," man could "solve the problems which everywhere confront him,"[11] Beard saw in the rise of trusts the death of free economic competition and the harbinger of new forms of combination in which "the people, instead of a few capitalists, will reap the benefits."[12] Man had only to give up his sham battles with "ancient devils, fog giants, metaphysical dragons" and apply his common sense to the problem of "social health" in order to secure an

8. This material on Beard's early career is drawn from *Current Biography* (1941), pp. 51–4; Merle Curti, "A Great Teacher's Teacher," *Social Education, 13* (1949), 263–6, 274; Harlan B. Phillips, "Charles Beard, Walter Vrooman, and the Founding of Ruskin Hall," *South Atlantic Quarterly, 50* (1951), 186–91; Beard, "Ruskin and the Babble of Tongues," *New Republic, 87* (1936), 370–2.

9. Beard, "Co-operation and the New Century," *Young Oxford, 2* (1900), 100.

10. *The Industrial Revolution*, pref. F. York Powell (London, Sonnenschein, 1901), p. 86.

11. Ibid., p. 31.

12. Ibid., p. 53.

equitable distribution of the necessities and opportunities of life.[13] In modern technology, substituting "the tireless power of Nature" for manual labor, he would find "the material key to man's spiritual progress."[14] In this spirit of reformist zeal and optimistic rationalism, which links the young graduate student with the old historian, Beard returned to America to finish his graduate work at Columbia University.

In Beard's soul the conscience of the reformer and the mind of the scholar lived, like the lion and the lamb, in uneasy peace. Perhaps his English experience had discouraged the simple expectations of the crusader, and so the intellectual curiosity of the historian had assumed dominance. In any event his doctor's thesis was a detached and impersonal study, written in the conventional spirit of political formalism: "The Office of Justice of the Peace in England in Its Origin and Development" (1904). But there were new intellectual forces stirring at Columbia, and Beard, as a professor of politics, soon found himself in a congenial atmosphere in which Robinson, Barnes, and Dewey all voiced the antiformalist mood. After Beard left Columbia, protesting the curtailment of academic freedom in war time, he joined them in setting up the New School for Social Research, which provided a rostrum not only for themselves but for the mordant iconoclast Thorstein Veblen, famous for his brilliant attacks on the arid formalism of the deductive school of classical economics. At Columbia, too, Beard enjoyed the friendship of E. R. A. Seligman, an economist whose book *The Economic Interpretation of History* became a primary source for Beard's economic determinism as applied to the Founding Fathers. This philosophy of history, as Richard Hofstadter has pointed out, had a strong appeal to intellectuals who had grown up in an age conditioned by muckrakers whose goal was "the inside story" about bribery, rebates, bought franchises, and the sale of adulterated food. In a world of

13. Ibid., p. 91.
14. Ibid., p. 42.

political bosses, economic "robber barons," and crusading journalists it was natural for alert minds to think of reality in a special way: "It was rough and sordid; it was hidden, neglected, and, so to speak, off-stage; and it was essentially a stream of external and material events, of which psychic events were a kind of pale reflex."[15] By 1906, as editor of an anthology of English historians, Beard declared that to study the past century of British political history without its economic foundations was to miss "the underlying forces of modern history."[16] In words prophetic of his treatment of the Founding Fathers he warned that legends about the sacred liberties of British freemen arose from a confusion of "class rights with supposedly 'national' rights."[17] Beard's economic determinism was fast forming in his mind before he turned his attention to the American past.

His approach to American history was a conscious challenge to earlier conceptions. He felt that the pietistic tendency to see events as the manifestation of some higher power was useless because it offered general, wholesale answers for specific, retail problems. Appeals to Providence explained everything in general without explaining anything in particular. He was no less dissatisfied with the "germ theory of politics," which, by tracing democratic institutions back to German folk communities, ignored concrete historical circumstances to focus on fuzzy abstractions about the Anglo-Saxon "racial spirit." Finally, Ranke's influence had nourished documentary analysis and classification without advancing any technique of historical explanation. The time had come for testing a new philosophy designed to fulfill the promise of the antiformalist tradition. "The theory of economic determinism has not been tried out in American history, and until it is tried out, it cannot be found

---

15. Richard Hofstadter, "Beard and the Constitution," *American Quarterly,* 2 (1950), 208.

16. *An Introduction to the English Historians* (New York, Macmillan, 1906), p. 506.

17. Ibid., p. 78.

wanting."[18] In this bold but pragmatic tone Beard prefaced one of the most controversial and influential pieces of historical writing ever to disturb the American mind—*An Economic Interpretation of the Constitution of the United States.*

The storm that broke in 1913 over this book has shrouded it in a false aura of melodrama and sensationalism. Beard felt his own work only gave a powerful fillip to a movement already under way among historians to "turn away from barren 'political' history to a study of the real economic forces which condition great movements in politics."[19] He took great pains to cite a long list of precursors in the antiformalist approach. Beard himself, three years before, in his *American Government and Politics,* had presented the American Revolution as an economic struggle against British mercantilism and had stressed the central role of traders, financiers, and manufacturers in the movement for the Constitution, pointing out that the framers were especially fearful for the rights of private property against the "levelling tendencies of propertyless masses."[20] Economic determinism, according to the Marxian formula, had even been sweepingly applied to the whole of American history in 1911 by Algie M. Simons' *Social Forces in American History.* But, as Becker remarked, Simons, writing "without fear and without research," had produced a history useful only as a handbook for doctrinaire socialists.[21] The novelty of Beard's book was not that it approached American heroes with something other than pious awe, or emphasized economic forces, or used the theory of economic determinism. His originality lay in his effort to demonstrate the relevance of the general theory by rigorous research into a central event in American history, presenting his findings in the spirit of the scholar

18. *An Economic Interpretation of the Constitution of the United States* (New York, Macmillan, 1913), p. 7.

19. Ibid., p. v.

20. *American Government and Politics* (New York, Macmillan, 1910), p. 47.

21. Becker, "The Reviewing of Historical Books," *Annual Report,* American Historical Association (1912), p. 133.

with no practical, political cause to defend. When the editor of *The Intercollegiate Socialist* queried him about his attitude toward socialism in 1913, Beard urged students to take an "intelligent interest" in such an important matter, but he did not commit himself to any political ideology or program.[22] His book had in no sense been written for the occasion and with reference to immediate controversies, he wrote many years later in a preface to the second edition, but the implications of his thesis could not be discussed disinterestedly in the disturbed political atmosphere of 1913. At a time when the Constitution was being democratized by amendments for the popular election of senators and the imposition of an income tax, only a year after Theodore Roosevelt, as leader of the Progressive party, had defended the recall of judicial decisions, a book which underlined the property-minded, undemocratic outlook of the Founding Fathers was bound to become controversial. For all his profound concern for contemporary history Beard tried to preserve a scholar's detachment amid the contention he had provoked by refusing a request to appear before the New York Bar Association to discuss judicial issues.[23]

The public clamor was, however, partly due to the inner ambiguity of Beard's treatment of the framers. Progressives and socialists, eager to justify their desires to reform American institutions, could pointedly cite his conclusion that most of the members of the Convention were "immediately, directly, and personally interested in the outcome of their labors at Philadelphia, and were to a greater or less extent economic beneficiaries from the adoption of the Constitution."[24] Why should a present generation, in need of social changes,

22. "Why Study Socialism?" *The Intercollegiate Socialist,* 1 (Spring–Summer, 1913), 3. Beard also wrote an article on the creation of American character by economic processes for another socialist magazine: "Internationalism in the United States," *New Review, 3* (August 1, 1915), 159–60.

23. *An Economic Interpretation of the Constitution of the United States* (2d ed. New York, Macmillan, 1939), pp. v–viii.

24. Ibid. (1913), p. 149.

be inhibited by reverence for a document that was only the instrument of capitalistic aggrandizement? Conservatives, on the other hand, could find comfort (though few of them did) in his defense of Alexander Hamilton as a man swayed by "large policies of government—not by any of the personal interests so often ascribed to him"[25] and in his praise of Robert Morris—representative of speculative land operators, the holders of securities, the dealers in public paper, and the mercantile groups seeking protection for manufactures—as a great statesman. Morris represented "every movable property interest in the country," thus symbolizing the economic forces which, according to Beard's thesis, had made the Constitution, yet Beard said of him: "It seems fair to say that no man contributed more to the establishment of our Constitution and the stability of our national institutions than Robert Morris, 'the Patriot Financier.' "[26] At least one conservative, Supreme Court Justice Sutherland, found Beard's book useful in 1933 to support a vigorous dissent from a decision upholding a state mortgage moratorium law, passed in the interests of debtors. Defending the sanctity of private contracts, the Justice found abundant evidence in the book designed to prove that the Constitution was made in order to prevent debtor legislation from threatening propertied and creditor interests.[27] If Beard was usually acclaimed by reformers and derided by conservatives, his thesis could be used for either cause.

He was convinced that economic determinism protected the historian from giving vent to a puritanical tendency to mete out salvation and damnation in his treatment of historical problems. He was determined to view the structure of classes and their conflict with all the cold neutrality of a disciple of Ranke. Of the economic struggle over the Constitution, dividing its friends from its foes, he said: "It is idle to inquire whether the rapacity of the creditors or the total depravity of the debtors . . . was responsible for this deep

25. Ibid., p. 114.
26. Ibid., pp. 135–6.
27. *Home Building and Loan Association v. Blaisdell* (1933) 290 U.S. 458–459, n. 3.

and bitter antagonism. It is sufficient for our purposes to discover its existence and to find its institutional reflex in the Constitution."[28] If Beard was a Marxist, it was only in the sense that he believed " 'those transformations in the structure of society which themselves condition the relations of social classes and the various manifestations of social life' " must be traced "in the last instance" to economic causes. This proposition, which he quoted from Seligman's exposition of the economic interpretation of history, was, he felt, "as nearly axiomatic as any proposition in social science" could be.[29] Though his defensive tactic of appealing to the Founding Fathers themselves, especially James Madison, as the source of his economic determinism was somewhat disingenuous, the strategy had the merit of pointing up Beard's opposition to the political and ethical views of Marxism. Unlike Marx, who believed the state would wither away in the classless society, he saw the conflict of interests in society as perpetual and defended the independent existence of individual and group economic interests over against the state as a necessary bulwark of constitutional government. Like the Founding Fathers, he attacked Rousseau as a dangerous propagandist for the tyranny of a numerical majority.[30] Whatever radicals may have concluded from Beard's study of the Constitution, he made it clear in his later writings that for him property rights were fundamental and sacred, and he felt that the Supreme Court's power of judicial review—a prime evil in the eyes of radical reformers—had a great and salutary political function in the American system.[31]

28. *An Economic Interpretation of the Constitution of the United States* (1913), p. 32.

29. Ibid., p. 15, n. 1.

30. *The Economic Basis of Politics* (3d ed. rev. New York, Knopf, 1945), pp. 53–4, 69–70, 113. For Beard's citation of non-Marxist sources of his economic approach see "That Noble Dream," *AHR, 41* (1935), 85.

31. Charles A. and Mary R. Beard, *American Citizenship* (New York, Macmillan, 1914), p. 54; Beard, *Contemporary American History 1877–1913* (New York, Macmillan, 1914), p. 87; Beard, *The Supreme Court and the Constitution* (New York, Macmillan, 1912), pp. 1–2. Cf. Robert E. Thomas, "A Reappraisal of Charles A. Beard's *An Economic Interpretation of the Constitution of the United States*," *AHR, 58* (1952), 370–5.

Yet for all his proclamations of objectivity and neutrality, Beard's handling of the economic interpretation was invidiously ambiguous. Seligman's theory, like that of Marx and Engels, condemned the simplistic notion of an economic man everywhere pursuing his private economic interests. Noneconomic forces played an important role in historical struggles and often a preponderant one in determining their *form;* economic necessity asserted itself only *in the last resort.*[32] Beard seemed to share this point of view when he warned his readers that the purpose of his inquiry was not to show that the Constitution was made for "the personal benefit of the members of the Convention." His point was that, instead of working "under the guidance of abstract principles of political science," they represented distinct groups, "whose economic interests they understood and felt in concrete, definite form through their own personal experience with identical property rights."[33] But in the first chapter, presenting his approach to history as a needed corrective of earlier conceptions, he cited "the economic advantages which the beneficiaries expected would accrue to themselves first" as "the direct, impelling motive" of the leaders of the historic movement for the Constitution.[34] He hardly clarified his purpose when he noted that " 'bare-faced selfishness' was not monopolized by Gerry in the Convention."[35] This underlying insinuation that the framers were intent on lining their pockets through the new government to be established by their labors was what made his book, despite its colorless impersonality of style, so sensational. SCAVENGERS HYENA-LIKE DESECRATE THE GRAVES OF THE DEAD PATRIOTS WE REVERE was the indignant headline judgment of the Marion *Star,* and even the unruffled Olympian, Justice Oliver Wendell Holmes,

---

32. E. R. A. Seligman, *The Economic Interpretation of History* (New York, Columbia University Press, 1902), p. 153.
33. *An Economic Interpretation of the Constitution of the United States,* p. 73.
34. Ibid., pp. 17–18.
35. Ibid., p. 98, n. 1.

was moved by Beard's "belittling innuendo" to protest that "high-mindedness is not impossible to man."[36]

Though Holmes was himself an antiformalist student of the law, he believed that the framers as patriots "wanted to make a nation and invested (bet) on the belief that they would make one, not that they wanted a powerful government because they had invested." Curiously enough, Beard's argument for the hypothesis Holmes rejected rested ultimately upon the assumption that because the Fathers were men of such high character they could not possibly have been mere speculators. Beard's primary source for the security holdings of the members of the Convention was the Treasury Department record of the funding books of the new government established in 1789. He was compelled to conclude that the holders of the debt listed had either purchased their securities before the Convention of 1787 or while they were part of the new government, when their own influence as politicians would have helped determine the value of their holdings. His reason for thinking that the holdings must have been acquired before the creation of the new government was an odd one for an economic determinist: If the members of the Convention had not bought their government securities until they had begun to operate the new government, they would have been speculators. "But it is hardly to be supposed," he said, almost with indignation, "that many of them would sink to the level of mere speculators."[37] For the historian who had been excoriated as a hyena-like scavenger there was no doubt about

36. The headline is from the May 3, 1913, issue, as quoted by Eric F. Goldman, *Rendezvous with Destiny: A History of Modern American Reform* (New York, Knopf, 1952), p. 154. Holmes' statement is from a letter to Sir Frederick Pollock, June 20, 1928, reproduced in *The Mind and Faith of Justice Holmes*, ed. Max Lerner (Boston, Little Brown, 1943), p. 448.

37. *An Economic Interpretation of the Constitution of the United States*, p. 75, n. 3. The most devastating but strident challenging of Beard's thesis is Robert E. Brown, *Charles Beard and the Constitution: A Critical Analysis of "An Economic Interpretation of the Constitution,"* Princeton, Princeton University Press, 1956.

which hypothesis was correct: "Respect for the framers of the Constitution should impel us to choose the former alternative."[38] Thus did he appeal from the framers drunk to the framers sober in order finally to show that they were after all, if not drunk, at least slightly tipsy with economic interests!

Beard's inept handling of the economic interpretation had obscured his own deep respect for the Founding Fathers. In his earlier and later work, when he was less anxious to demonstrate the truth of economic determinism, his frank admiration of them was clearly manifest. He had also stressed the concern of the Convention for property rights in a general sense in his *American Government and Politics* (1910), but there he had pointed out that the framers had been faced with practical problems and their experience of popular assemblies had given them a natural fear of leveling attacks on the rights of minorities. In that book the Founding Fathers were presented as men of their age who were not modern democrats simply because the universal right of suffrage had not yet been accepted as a common ideal. If they had violated instructions to amend the Articles of Confederation by writing a new Constitution, they had not been conspirators, but merely loyal to the cause of national union. He had, in fact, profound respect for such a long-lived document, made in a century which saw scores of paper constitutions dismally fail, and for its makers, unsurpassed in any assembly for richness in political experience, practical knowledge, and profound insight into the sources of human action and power.[39] By 1937 he could forthrightly praise the public-spirited men who founded government on the new basis of "social purpose," instead of on class rights, and as "public personages embued with a deep sense of social responsibility" staked their lives and fortunes on the independence and security of the Republic.[40] In *The Republic* (1943)

38. *Economic Origins of Jeffersonian Democracy* (New York, Macmillan, 1915), p. 106, n. 1.

39. *American Government and Politics*, pp. 45–50.

40. Beard, *The Unique Function of Education in American Democracy*, Educational Policies Commission (Washington, 1937), pp. 10–11.

and his *Basic History of the United States* (1944) the Founding Fathers are no longer the Funding Fathers; they are proponents of national unity and constitutional government.[41] Yet in 1913 his simplistic use of economic determinism, his ambiguity about motivation, and his failure to give the framers' political ideas a historical setting in the climate of opinion made it appear as if he were saying in muted language what socialists like Simons had outrightly declared: that the Constitution was formulated in secret session by a conspiratorial body that had forced upon a disfranchised people, through a dishonest rigging of the voting system, a document designed to protect a small group of wealthy rulers.[42] If Beard's methods were thoroughly unsensational, the effect of his book was unintentionally melodramatic. As a gadfly to respectable opinion, he must have been amused by the hysterical comment he had provoked. The New York *Times* greeted his resignation from the university as "Columbia's Deliverance," and there arose the celebrated story that when President Butler was asked if he had read Beard's last book, he replied fervently, "I hope so."

In his succeeding books Beard tried to make it clear that he was not engaged in grinding anybody's axe, nor was he applying European ideology to American facts. It was Turner who provided him with the motto for his *Economic Origins of Jeffersonian Democracy:* " 'We may trace the contest between the capitalist and the democratic pioneer from the earliest colonial days.' " Following this lead, Beard presented the rise of Jefferson's party as the coherent opposition of workers, farmers, and planters to capitalists, merchants, and manufacturers. But he was careful to emphasize that the voting in Congress on Hamilton's program reflected not the private economic interest of the members, but the interests of their constitu-

41. *The Republic: Conversations on Fundamentals* (New York, Viking, 1943), p. 204; Charles A. and Mary R. Beard, *A Basic History of the United States* (New York, Doubleday Doran, 1944), p. 125.

42. Cf. Simons, *Social Forces in American History* (New York, Macmillan, 1911), p. 99.

encies. The issue was not one of character or its corruption but of
the collision of economic forces—fluid capital versus agrarianism.
From his point of view both interests were legitimate.[43] Jefferson,
in Beard's account, was no hero of the virtuous underdogs; his
democratic outlook was described as "a class faith and his appeal
was a class appeal."[44]

If Beard was frankly Marxist in making exploitation the origin
of the state and class rule, he refused to get involved in an "intermi-
nable argument" about the economic interpretation of history. In
characteristically pragmatic tones he disdained theoretical questions
about his book, content that "men of a practical turn of mind will
be satisfied with its significance in the world of fact."[45] For him
there was nothing invidious about recognizing that politics in
American history had not been controlled by "any fine-spun theories
of political science." If Hamilton had induced security-holding
capitalists to support the government by a fiscal program catering
to their interests, the policy showed his wisdom, because government could not rest on "the platonic support of genial well-
wishers."[46] In the economic interpretation Beard found an escape
from the pieties and legalisms of an earlier generation of historians.
In the end, of course, his skeptical inquiries into the assumptions of
the scientific historians were to have effect on his own commitment
to economic determinism, but, for the time being, he stuck to it as
a practical principle of historical synthesis.

At its best, Beard's massive The Rise of American Civilization, a
multivolumed work of impressive scope, written in collaboration
with his wife, put into practice the relative flexibility and subtlety
of the economic interpretation of history as defined by Seligman.
Beard made it clear that he did not believe in the fiction of an abstract
economic man forever pursuing his economic interests. Even groups

43. *Economic Origins of Jeffersonian Democracy*, p. 195.
44. Ibid., p. 428.
45. Ibid., p. 435.
46. Ibid., p. 131.

with similar interests might reason differently about how to satisfy them, so that the boundaries of class lines would never be neat and rigid.[47] Thus he presented the American Revolution not as the consequence of a precise calculation of profits and losses, registered in ledgers, but as a conflict of tempers and ideas, arising out of economic antagonisms, "in the last analysis." Human motives could not be exhausted by the cash nexus; indeed, he saw religious faith, desire for adventure, flight from slavery, restlessness, and sheer curiosity at work in the movement for colonizing America. Ideas too, in his story, had their own force, for whatever changes took place in the economic and social structure of the country, the Enlightenment philosophy of human rights and equality would, he felt, have transformed the intellectual climate of the age; and moral sentiments were the driving force behind the Abolitionist crusade against slavery.[48]

Yet, whatever recognition Beard gave to noneconomic motives and forces, The Rise of American Civilization vibrates with the strength of his conviction that, as he wrote of the Civil War, "the core of the vortex" lay "in the flowing substance of things limned by statistical reports on finance, commerce, capital, industry, railways, and agriculture" or other "prosaic muniments."[49] His history thus minimized the political issues of the Revolution, discounted the controversy over slavery as a precipitant of the Civil War, explained the origins of the 14th Amendment in terms of a conspiracy to create an instrument of corporate privilege, and insinuated that President Wilson had been strongly influenced by advice to intervene on the side of the Allies in the first World War in order to maintain our trade position and avert a panic.[50] In all these interpre-

47. "The Economic Basis of Politics," New Republic, 32 (1922), 128–9; The American Party Battle (New York, Macmillan, 1928), p. 11.

48. The Rise of American Civilization, 1, 196, 10, 725, 699.

49. Ibid., 2, 54.

50. Ibid., 1, 201; 2, 39–40, 111–14; America in Midpassage, Vol. 3 of The Rise of American Civilization (New York, Macmillan, 1939), 1, 416–17.

tations, now under heavy fire from contemporary historians, Beard was led by his theory to find, "in the last instance," a final economic cause. Charged with something of the force of a tragic drama, his narrative, with magnificent sweep and power, records the reign of economic Necessity, entangling man remorselessly in an inexorable process beyond the will of any man or group of men, which neither the learned nor the great can anticipate or control: "All were caught up and whirled in a blast too powerful for their wills, too swift for their mental operations. . . . Such havoc does fate play with the little schemes of men!"[51]

Through Beard's eyes we see the course of events in a pattern almost as schematic as the Marxist vision of an unfolding dialectic. The American Revolution becomes only a battle in a war of forces waged "for more than two centuries on this continent"—the conflict between province and metropolis which has "figured in every great national crisis from that day to this."[52] We see that the triumph of business enterprise is entailed in the irresistible development of that event which he had made the prophetic theme of his first book—the Industrial Revolution: "In this titanic process, disputes over slavery and even the Civil War itself were incidents that delayed but did not halt the giant of steam in his seven-league boots."[53] After the war, the conflict between business and agriculture, as ancient as civilization itself, only serves to show that "History was repeating old patterns in a new and majestic setting."[54] Thereafter, in Beard's story, American history is compared to the Roman Empire. The postwar plutocrats are described looting Europe just as the parvenues of Rome in Cicero's day ransacked Greece and Egypt. Hearst and Pulitzer, the aggressive editors, are New World Caesars, and Bryan and Franklin D. Roosevelt become reincarnations of Gaius Gracchus. American imperialism in 1899

51. *The Rise of American Civilization*, 2, 62, 544. Cf. ibid., 1, 596.
52. Ibid., 1, 202.
53. Ibid., p. 662.
54. Ibid., 2, 166.

echoes the state of the Roman Republic in 242 B.C. at the end of the Punic War. Labor leaders, like Gompers and Powderly, agrarian champions, like Bryan, and critics of plutocracy, like Henry Adams and Theodore Roosevelt, are said to have their counterparts in the plebeian and patrician protests of Cato, Cicero, and Juvenal against the rich barbarians of Rome. As Beard's tale progresses it becomes clear that even if there was no Cataline in Coolidge's Administration, the hour is approaching when the union of money lenders, politicians, and military men in America will mark the time at which the doom of the Roman Empire was at hand. Relentlessly, Beard pursued his analogy into the crash of 1929: "The mightiest Julius had fallen and 'the sheeted dead did squeak and gibber in the Roman streets.' "55

For all its force as a literary device Beard's unifying metaphor dramatically brings to light the dangers implicit in economic determinism. Though he once was quoted as saying, "Of the totality of things discussed knowingly by the Bright Boys, I am entirely ignorant,"56 his practice of history tended to reinstate the conception of the course of events as the working out of some grand scheme. If he had rejected the vision of history as a plot controlled by the moving finger of Providence, whether in pietistic or scientific terms, his economic interpretation created what appears to be only a secularized version of it. Historical forces thus turn into abstractions, ghosts that terrorize events, and the historical process is hypostatized into a mysterious necessity independent of human will and concrete circumstances. On Beard's stage men and events seem like puppets, manipulated by the master forces of business and agriculture, eternally conflicting in a sterile, mechanical dialectic. From this point of view history is arbitrarily fissured into a realm of appearance and a realm of reality, but the reality is vouched for not so much by empirical evidence as by the tyrannous demands of an a priori theory. Though economic determinism allows complexity

55. *America in Midpassage,* 1, 60.
56. *Current Biography* (1941), p. 54.

at the level of motivation and with respect to the form of historical stuggles, the dogma of a final economic explanation, "in the last analysis," denies complexity at the level of large-scale crises, where it is most needed. Under the seductive allure of the theory the historian always finds in the end the simplicity he originally disavows.

These defects inherent in economic determinism are especially crippling to the historian who, like Beard, would try to interpret cultural developments. Beard believed that art, religion, and learning are "bent to the order in which they thrive and have meaning and vitality only in relation to their economic substructure."[57] Thus he did not tarry over the mere "logical devices" of the English Puritans, for example, because in his view their theology was only a "defense mechanism" for men nurtured on the Bible who wished to resist taxation.[58] In this way the complex problem of the relation between religion and politics is "solved" by a process of simplification in which one is made a superficial function of the other. This mood of tough-mindedness was more at home in the market place and the forum than in the salons of culture; and though much praised in his day by reformers, it shared the businessman's scorn for cultural fiddling while Rome burned. Philistines might well have applauded Beard's admiration for William Cullen Bryant as "a solid citizen" who was no "languid aesthete at home amid the perfumes of a salon sustained by fixed investments," and also have heartily sympathized with his thinly veiled contempt for Henry James, "a whole generation removed from the odors of the shop."[59] Beard's treatment of cultural history often gave the impression that "The Sage of New Milford" was a kind of Connecticut Yankee at King Arthur's Court.

57. Introduction, *Whither Mankind: A Panorama of Modern Civilization*, ed. Beard (New York, Longmans Green, 1928), p. 13.

58. *The Rise of American Civilization*, 1, 31. Contrast his *An Introduction to the English Historians*, p. 321.

59. *The Rise of American Civilization*, 1, 793; 2, 441. Cf. his praise of Steinbeck and denigration of Cather, *America in Midpassage*, 2, 631-2, 659.

In the early 1930's Beard's inquiries into the foundations of historical knowledge forced him to reassess the economic determinism which had provided him so long with a unifying theory. He was compelled now to come to terms with his own skepticism, which had already blasted the determinism of scientific history. In sharp contrast to his use of analogies with Roman history in *The Rise of American Civilization,* he announced in 1936 that social uniformities are not stable and do not repeat themselves eternally: "only scholasticism can imagine that the social realities of ancient Rome and contemporary America to which they give the same names are the same, are identical."[60] Stimulated by his reading of Kurt Riezler and Karl Mannheim, Beard affirmed that ideas change through internal compulsions and under inner examination, not merely from the impact of material interests, just as these in turn are transformed by ideas.[61] In a school text he wrote with his wife in 1937 he put his new belief into practice by pointing out that what men thought and did about political, social, and economic affairs depended in considerable measure upon their knowledge of science, letters, and the arts, even upon their religion and ethics.[62] Revising his *The Economic Basis of Politics* in 1945, he reminded his readers that the old English and American idea that power followed property could be true only in a free society where the absence of political and military despotism provided scope for the conflict of economic interests.[63] The rise of fascism in Europe had been a response to forces which a merely economic interpretation could not grasp, as he had good reason to know since he had formerly shrugged off the "ethics and verbal flourishes" of communism and fascism, convinced that European society was assimilating itself to American civilization by

60. *The Discussion of Human Affairs* (New York, 1936), p. 56.

61. Beard and Alfred Vagts, "Currents of Thought in Historiography," *AHR,* 42 (1937), 479.

62. *The Making of American Civilization* (New York, Macmillan, 1937), p. vi.

63. *The Economic Basis of Politics,* pp. 90-1.

a similar dedication to the goal of "mechanical comfort and prosperity for the masses."[64]

Yet what stands out in all this philosophical soul-searching is Beard's plain reluctance to abandon economic determinism. Though his revolt against scientific history led him to conclude that picking out causes from the seamless web of history was an expression only of the historian's values and interests, nevertheless, in a preface to a new edition of his famous study of the Constitution published in 1935, he still spoke of "great transformations in society" being produced by "primordial or fundamental" economic forces which "come nearer 'explaining' events than any other 'forces.' "[65] For all his avowed ignorance of "the totality of things discussed knowingly by the Bright Boys," he tried in his *The Discussion of Human Affairs*, after destructive criticism of scientific history, to propound a general theory of the historical process—a "realistic dialectics" of ideas and interests, evolving together in time and related to basic economic conditions. Despite his skeptical relativism, he still wanted to "grapple with the total situation" without making "value judgments."[66] Even Beard's skepticism could not finally inhibit that impulse he shared with both Henry Adams and Karl Marx to find a master key that would unlock the secrets of history.

If Beard did not have the confidence of an Adams or a Marx that he could solve the "riddle of the universe" by providing "an assured prediction" of the future course of history, he was, nevertheless, committed to an "act of faith" in progress upward toward an ideal goal. In his first book, written as a young graduate student in England, he had pointed to the promise implicit in the life and work of James Watt that science and technology would give man the power

---

64. *The Rise of American Civilization*, 2, 777–8.

65. *An Economic Interpretation of the Constitution of the United States* (2d ed. New York, 1939), p. xii. Cf. Beard, "Historiography and the Constitution," *The Constitution Reconsidered*, ed. Conyers Read (New York, Columbia University Press, 1938), p. 164.

66. *The Discussion of Human Affairs*, p. 116.

to control his destiny. As president of the American Political Science Association in 1926, Beard proposed modern technology as the means of implementing the idea of indefinite progress sketched by the Abbé de Saint-Pierre in the 18th century. If, as a skeptic, Beard was prepared to admit that the past was "without order or design," he was nevertheless still "haunted by the shadowing thought that by immense efforts of will and intelligence, employing natural science as the supreme instrumentality of power, mankind may rise above necessity into the kingdom of freedom, subduing material things to humane and rational purposes."[67] With a radiant glow of optimistic rationalism he closed the second volume of his *The Rise of American Civilization* on a note of unquestioned assurance in "the continuous fulfillment" of the historic idea of unlimited progress:

> Concretely it meant an invulnerable faith in democracy, in the ability of the undistinguished masses, as contrasted with heroes and classes, to meet by reasonably competent methods the issues raised in the flow of time—a faith in the efficacy of that new and mysterious instrument of the modern mind, "the invention of invention," moving from one technological triumph to another . . . effecting an ever wider distribution of the blessings of civilization . . . and through the cumulative forces of intellectual and artistic reactions, conjuring from the vasty deeps of the nameless and unknown creative imagination of the noblest order, subduing physical things to the empire of the spirit—doubting not the capacity of the Power that had summoned into being all patterns of the past and present, living and dead, to fulfill its endless destiny.[68]

67. Beard, Intro. to J. B. Bury, *The Idea of Progress: An Inquiry into Its Growth and Origin* (New York, Macmillan, 1932), p. xl. For other affirmations by Beard of the idea of progress see "Time, Technology, and the Creative Spirit in Political Science," *American Political Science Review, 21* (1927), 5, and "A Historian's Quest for Light," *Proceedings of the Association of History Teachers of the Middle States and Maryland, 29* (1931), 21.

68. *The Rise of American Civilization, 2, 831.*

The Great Depression, coming only two years after he had written this purple peroration, heralding "the dawn and not the dusk of the gods," made it clear that if he could call spirits from the vasty deep, they would not come when called. Yet Beard never wavered in his faith in the idea of progress. As a "tough-minded" antiformalist, convinced that American life has always been "in the main hard, economic and realistic—a conquest of material things," he was sure that progress would be materialistic, "mass progress, measurable in averages and susceptible of graphic presentation."[69] The economy of abundance was "The Promise of American Life." This goal could be obtained by planning, that talisman of rationalistic politics. He had himself observed the power of planning when he had gone to Tokyo at the Home Minister's request to advise on municipal politics during the reconstruction of the city after the earthquake of 1923. There the vision seemed almost a reality, and when the depression struck America, Beard set to work to draw up a Five-Year Plan to bring into existence the economy of abundance in a collectivist democracy by a centralization of authority adequate to control the planless irrationality of the market place.[70]

Beard had once defined the great historian as a man of faith who cast the weft of the future through the warp of the past by an act of prophetic discernment: he was now prepared to qualify for the role himself. With increasing passion his historical work became a tendentious argument for the necessity of fulfilling "The Promise of American Life." The acid of his skepticism had corroded the hard dogmas of economic determinism, but his "act of faith" in history

69. "That Promise of American Life," *New Republic, 81* (1935), 352; Intro. to Bury, p. xxv.

70. Intro. to *Toward Civilization*, ed. Beard (New York, Longmans Green, 1930), p. 17; "A 'Five-Year' Plan for America," *Forum, 86* (1931), 1–11; "A Search for the Center," *Scribner's, 91* (January 1932), 2–7; *The Open Door at Home: A Trial Philosophy of National Interest*, collab. G. H. E. Smith (New York, 1935), pp. 216 ff.

as an upward progress toward an ideal gave him another lever and a new place to stand from which to move the world. In accordance with his own belief in the historian as a statesman without portfolio, he raked the American past for "a body of professed values appropriate and indispensable to new policy—values abundant in literature and faith, and realized here and there in practice."[71] This quest produced the final volume in his series on the rise of American Civilization, *The American Spirit: A Study of the Idea of Civilization in the United States* (1942). Condemning the abstractions of both "economic man" and "machine man," he appealed instead to the idea of progress advanced in Europe by the *philosophes* of the Enlightenment and realized in America by the great republican statesmen of the 18th century. In this vision of progress Beard's passionate moral sense, which had so eagerly responded to Ruskin when he read him at DePauw, found release.

Despite its dogmatic rigidities Beard's earlier economic determinism had at least represented an effort to avoid the moralistic distortions of a Manichaean approach to history. But now his "act of faith" had eliminated any checkrein. In *The American Spirit* he found the impetus to betterment in two traditions, one for domestic, the other for foreign affairs. The hope of progress lay with the critics of the unregulated market, from the Quaker John Woolman to the utopian novelist Edward Bellamy, and with the critics of internationalism and imperialism, from the isolationist Founding Fathers to the intellectuals of the Anti-imperialist League. Thus did his picture of the American past take on the characteristics of a morality play—a Manichaean conflict between democrats committed to nationalism and equalitarianism, and capitalists devoted to acquisition and war. In this melodrama Europe was but a malignant chorus, confusing Americans with Freudianism, Catholicism, and Marxism, ideas derived from reactionary, hierarchical societies, doomed to be forever beyond the pale of progress. If he

71. *The Open Door at Home*, p. 152.

officially believed there was "no final act for the drama of history,"[72] he became, increasingly, the passionate spokesman for a collectivist democracy, isolated from the rest of the world, as a fulfillment of his dream of utopia. He thus became the most striking and influential American example of what Herbert Butterfield has called "the Whig interpretation of history," which menaces historical understanding by overdramatizing the conflicts of the past into a struggle between progressives and reactionaries and organizing them upon an unfolding principle of progress. Beard's revision of economic determinism, though certainly necessary, had, ironically, fostered the very fallacies that theory had been designed to avoid.

Whatever may be said about the limitations of Beard's economic interpretation of history, he brought to the American past the "tyrannous eye" Emerson had called for. Informed by an instinctive knowledge of "the value of our incomparable materials," and a hearty taste for "the barbarism and materialism of the times," Beard's imagination grasped Emerson's point that "banks and tariffs, the newspaper and caucus, Methodism and Unitarianism, are flat and dull to dull people, but rest on the same foundations of wonder as the town of Troy and temple of Delphi, and are as swiftly passing away."[73] Eventually and understandably he came to feel that the stream of history could not be adequately fished with the mesh of economic determinism. Yet his commitment to the idea of progress was not a principle of explanation for the historical past; it was a heroic attempt to control the historical future. What would he do if history abandoned him to faith in a lost cause? Being no longer an economic determinist, how would he explain such a shocking turn of events? "I was right in saying that the war was on the way," he wrote a friend after the United States had become

72. Charles A. and Mary R. Beard, *The American Spirit: A Study of the Idea of Civilization in the United States,* Vol. *4* of The Rise of American Civilization, pp. 532–3.

73. Ralph Waldo Emerson, "The Poet," *Essays, Second Series,* Standard Library Edition, *3* (Boston, Houghton Mifflin, 1883), 40.

fully engaged in the second World War, "but I was foolish in laying such emphasis on economic aspects of the business. Man hasn't sense enough to pursue economic interests consistently." To him the war was proof that "man seems bound to have a berserk rage every so often—a senseless berserk rage, and I regard it as a mistake to gloss that fact over."[74] The note of bitterness provokes a question which haunts the last phase of his career: if the historical scene seemed dark to him, was it only because human reason had generally suffered an eclipse, or had the light of historical understanding in the historian himself also begun to flicker? Beard had found economic determinism wanting. He was also to discover that his faith in the idea of rational progress, when sent to the school of modern history, would be forced to learn hard lessons from an exacting teacher.

74. Letter to O. G. Villard, July 18 [1945?], Villard Papers.

PART THREE

Liberals in Crisis

In the political conflicts of their age Carl Becker and Charles Beard found a rugged testing-ground for their philosophies. As pragmatic relativists, for whom ideas were weapons in the struggles of history, they had no desire to stand on the sidelines; yet, as anti-formalists, distrustful of institutional forms and political theories, they could not easily meet the ideological challenge of fascism and communism. Their own ideology of liberalism, one might think, should have given them sufficient armor to meet the totalitarian attack on civil liberties and constitutional democracy, but with them liberalism itself had lost many of its intellectual underpinnings. In the general erosion of fixed standards through the impact of historical relativism they were forced to search for solid ground upon which to stand, and, despite their revolt against scientific history, they clung to science and technology as the instruments of salvation, the modern means of fulfilling the old faith of liberalism in the idea of progress.

If Becker and Beard shared with Dewey, Veblen, Robinson, and Barnes a "tough-minded" empiricism, designed to liberate thought from the "tender-minded" formalism and rationalism of traditional philosophy, their common devotion to an ideology of scientific progress was the "tender-minded" other side of their empirical "tough-mindedness."[1] Though Reason, in their view, did not come trailing clouds of glory, the Golden Age was all the more glorious for being anticipated in tomorrow's sunrise when the rationality implicit in science and technology would at last control society.

1. For an account of the general antiformalist movement see Morton G. White, *Social Thought in America: The Revolt against Formalism*, New York, Viking, 1949; I have tried to bring out the utopian strain in this movement in "The Twentieth-century Enlightenment," *American Political Science Review*, 49 (1955), 321–39.

This technocratic rationalism, which makes the mistake of attributing to tradition the rigidity that really characterizes the ideology of progress, was a poor chart for the rough waters of 20th-century history, bedeviled by disillusionment, depression, total war, and totalitarian terror. It led Becker, after an early disenchantment with the confident mood of Wilsonian democracy, to a troubled quest for some new foundation for the old liberal democracy whose traditional supports he no longer trusted, and by the time of the coming of the second World War he realized that his pragmatic relativism was an inadequate bulwark against the challenge of fascism. In his last two books he worked to promote a realistic confidence in the values of a free society because he was anxious to prevent that cycle of naïve hope and bitter despair he had himself experienced. With Beard disillusionment over Wilson's war policy came much later, but the scars went deeper, vividly marking the last decade of his stormy career when he became a passionate pleader for isolationism as the fulfillment of the idea of progress. The search of Becker and Beard for orientation in the crises of their age casts a harsh but revealing light on the plight of pragmatic relativism and antiformalism in a time of troubles.

CHAPTER SIX

The Dilemma of a Modern Diderot

IN 1915 Carl Becker confidently concluded his *Beginnings of the American People* with the judgment that the sweeping generalities of the Declaration of Independence had formulated "those basic truths which no criticism can seriously impair, and to which the minds of men must always turn, so long as faith in democracy shall endure."[1] Between 1915 and 1939 he experienced a trial of his own faith that shook his confidence in the "glittering generalities" of 18th-century liberalism. His intellectual odyssey has a special interest because of his persistent effort to ground his values on a philosophical basis and his willingness to follow the bent of the modern temper wherever it led him. What Hawthorne said of Melville applies also to Becker: "He can neither believe, nor be comfortable in his unbelief; and he is too honest and courageous not to try to do one or the other."[2] His spiritual dilemma had its origins in the contrast between his sympathy with the liberal values of the philosophers of the Enlightenment and his own skeptical outlook, which was hard pressed to give these values intellectual support. He had himself shown how the remnants of Christian faith and the metaphysical background of Newtonian physics had buttressed the Heavenly City of the 18th-century *philosophes*. Like them, he cherished Liberty, Equality, Fraternity, Humanity, Toleration, and

1. *Beginnings of the American People*, Riverside History of the United States, 1 (Boston, 1915), p. 253.
2. *The English Notebooks*, ed. Randall Stewart (New York, Modern Language Association, 1941), p. 433.

Reason, but putting these values in capitals did not remedy the difficulty that he had lost faith in the absolutes which had once upheld them. Yet he too wanted "to bring spiritual first aid to a harassed and perplexed generation."[3] In his own mind he suffered that tension between ethics and skepticism which he had recognized in 1915 to be "The Dilemma of Diderot."

The first World War was, as Becker pointed out, "a black backdrop on the stage of history, shutting out the past and throwing an ominous shadow on things present and to come."[4] When it came, he backed President Wilson's policy of intervention, convinced that the fight "to make the world safe for democracy" was a modern extension of the Monroe Doctrine's challenge to the autocratic powers of the Holy Alliance.[5] As a critic of the assumptions of scientific history, Becker also had a philosophical stake in the cause of the Allies. Historical determinism and the cult of amoral objectivity had led, he felt, to the pernicious doctrine that success is the only evidence of right. Ranke's spirit had its counterpart in the Machiavellian "realism" of German diplomats and generals. American intervention in the war gave to free men an opportunity to refute the "disastrous assumption," implicit in most 19th-century thought, that "man cannot by taking thought shape his own destiny, since he is himself only part and parcel of a natural process, inextricably enmeshed in the complexly threaded forces that uselessly move the cosmos along its uncharted course." In the deepest sense of all, he believed, it was a war "to reduce this philosophy to a reductio ad absurdum."[6] With these powerful convictions he went to Washington in 1918 to join other historians in writing propaganda

3. Becker, *Progress and Power* (Stanford, Stanford University Press, 1936), p. 9.

4. "What We Didn't Know Hurt Us a Lot," *Yale Review, 33* (1944), 394.

5. Becker, "The Monroe Doctrine and the War," *Minnesota History Bulletin, 2* (1917), 61–8.

6. "Tender and Tough-minded Historians," *Dial, 65* (1918), 108. Cf. "German Historians and the Great War," *Dial, 60* (1916), 163–4.

for the Committee on Public Information, producing two pamphlets designed to explain the German threat and American war aims.[7]

After the Peace Conference of Versailles, which shattered the hopes of many liberals for a new order based on Wilsonian principles, the president returned from Europe to lead his tragically unsuccessful crusade for American acceptance of the League of Nations, which to his mind justified whatever compromises he had been forced to make in the treaty. Becker was one of a group of historians who met with Wilson sometime after his return. Many years later, recalling the event, Becker wrote that the president seemed to him then to have been "a man at bay," fighting desperately for "the conviction that he hadn't wholly failed."[8] In Becker's judgment, as in that of many others, Wilson certainly had failed. He had not only compromised his principles; he had concealed the fact in a flood of self-righteous rhetoric, putting his name to a disingenuous treaty that had been conceived in hatred and imposed in vengeance.[9] No longer a missionary enterprise to defend democracy, the war had become, in Becker's eyes, "the most futile exhibition of unreason, take it all in all, ever made by civilized society," into which governments and peoples had rushed "with undiminished stupidity, with unabated fanaticism, with unimpaired capacity for deceiving themselves and others."[10]

Becker's skeptical temper, which colored the pragmatic relativism he proposed in opposition to the dogmas of scientific history, was heightened by his disenchantment with Wilson, the war, and the peace. To one of his friends he wrote bitterly in 1920: "I have always been susceptible to the impression of the futility of life, and always easily persuaded to regard history as no more than the meaningless

---

7. "German Attempts to Divide Belgium," *A League of Nations, 1* (1918), 307–42; *America's War Aims and Peace Plans,* War Information Series, 21, Washington, 1918.

8. Letter to Frederick Lewis Allen, March 19, 1933, Becker Papers.

9. Becker, "Mr. Wilson at the Peace Conference," *Nation, 116* (1923), 186.

10. "What Are Historical Facts?" *Western Political Quarterly, 8* (1955), 339.

resolution of blind forces which struggling men—good men and bad
—do not understand and cannot control, although they amuse themselves with the pleasing illusion that they do. The war and the peace
(God save the mark!) have only immensely deepened this pessimism."[11] American politics, reflecting a revulsion against idealism
and a quest for "normalcy," offered little to comfort the liberal
mind. Chauvinistic resentment of "hyphenated" ethnic groups during the war, drastic curtailment of free speech under the Espionage
Acts, arbitrary arrests and deportation of aliens in 1919, and the
Attorney General's provocation of hysteria over the "Red Scare"
of 1920 had seriously jeopardized civil liberties and the spirit of due
process of law. Faced with a listless campaign between the evasive
Harding and the uninspired Cox, Becker scarcely cared whether he
voted or not. The position of Eugene V. Debs as the Socialist party
candidate was at least distinctly different; serving sentence for
seditious speech, he was compelled to run his campaign from the
federal prison in Atlanta. "Therefore I voted for Debs," Becker
wryly remarked, "not because he was a Socialist, but because he
was in jail. . . . Such opportunities to vote intelligently are unfortunately rare."[12]

His mood found astringent expression in *The King of Beasts,* an
unpublished poetic fantasy, written as a children's story with a
satirical moral for adults, in the vein of Lewis Carroll. In this parable
the nations of the world appear in the guise of animals. The Eagle
presides at a Council of Force and Virtue and proposes to the assembly of large and small animals a Wilsonian compromise by
which "our enemies shall surrender their means of conflict that the

---

11. Letter to William E. Dodd, June 17, 1920, Becker Papers. Reprinted in
Phil Snyder, "Carl L. Becker and the Great War: A Crisis for a Humane Intelligence," *Western Political Quarterly, 9* (1956), 1–10.

12. "The Modern Leviathan," in *Everyman His Own Historian* (New York,
1935), p. 88. Early in 1920 he was quite willing to gamble on Hoover if he
should be nominated. Letter to Richard A. Newhall, March 24, 1920, Becker
Papers.

peace be not broken, while the Lion and the Tiger and the Eagle shall retain their means of conflict lest the peace be not kept. This is the first and greatest of the compromises, and upon this all the others depend."[13] After this stroke of high policy is made, the Dove of Peace is unveiled, lying on its back, feet in air, as if dead, or perhaps, as the Donkey remarks, only asleep. Yet even in 1920 Becker's capacity for self-criticism made him aware that much of his anger at Wilson was rooted in his own irritation at being "naive enough to suppose, during the war, that Wilson could ever accomplish those ideal objects which are so well formulated in his state papers."[14] Three years later he confessed that, having studied history for twenty-five years, he was angry at himself for not having realized that "after such a war the peace of Versailles was precisely what one might have expected." Being no party man with a cause to serve, but only a historian, "endeavoring to understand this damnable world," he put away his anger and charitably judged that if Wilson was wrong-headed, "he was wrong-headed in the right direction."[15] This inner poise, the discipline of a sensitive historical imagination, kept Becker from reacting to the revelations of secret treaties among the Allies and the subsequent controversy over the war-guilt question with the passionate indignation of some of the "revisionist" historians. If he had no quarrel with the argument of Harry Elmer Barnes, one of the pioneer "revisionists," that Austria, Russia, and France bore more guilt for starting the war than Germany, he did not share Barnes' melodramatic view of the diplomats and generals as "sinister conspirators" against mankind: "No more than other people did they undermine their self-respect by consciously engaging in evil practices."[16]

13. "The King of Beasts," MS, Becker Papers, p. 97.
14. Letter to William E. Dodd, June 17, 1920, Becker Papers.
15. Letter to William E. Dodd, February 26, 1923, Becker Papers.
16. "Assessing the Blame for the World War: A Symposium," *Current History, 20* (1924), 456. This is Becker's comment on Barnes, "Assessing the Blame for the World War," ibid., pp. 171–95. See also Becker's letter to Barnes, February 21, 1926, Becker Papers.

The collapse of Becker's wartime idealism would not, it seems clear, have led him very far down the road of disillusionment without the propulsion of deeper doubts generated by his philosophy itself. As an antiformalist, schooled by Turner, he saw "the secret of American history" in the persistence of democratic ideals flourishing in the primitive conditions of frontier society.[17] Yet he sensed the ominous implications of this thesis which Turner himself had failed to grasp, because, as Becker wrote Beard, Turner "was so in love with America and its ideas, that he clung to the notion that our blessed liberty, equality, and fraternity was not only something new in the world, but that it would always somehow remain what it was."[18] But Becker realized that, with the passing of free land in the 20th century, Turner's hypothesis implied that American democratic institutions and ideals had been the result of "a primitive, and therefore surely a passing stage of evolution."[19] After reading Beard's *The American Leviathan* he was more convinced than ever that Turner's optimism had been unjustified. Modern society, dominated by industrial and technological change, reduced politics to a process of impersonal functioning and adjustment. In the 20th century there was only government of the people, by the politicians, for whatever groups were powerful enough to get their way.[20]

Writing out of the depths of a national depression in 1932 Becker speculated on the fortunes of liberalism with modulated despair. Political liberty had fostered plutocracy; equality, championed by revolutionary socialists, had led to drastic curtailments of liberty.

17. Becker, *The United States: An Experiment in Democracy* (New York, Harper and Bros., 1920), p. 160.

18. Letter, n.d., shown to me through the courtesy of Dr. Alfred Vagts. Probably dated early in February 1939, since Beard's answer of February 4 seems to be about his essay on Turner written in February 1939 for the *New Republic*.

19. "Frederick Jackson Turner," *Everyman His Own Historian*, p. 226.

20. "The Modern Leviathan," ibid., p. 86.

Desiring both liberty and equality the liberal mind was poised on the horns of an agonizing dilemma. It could not choose liberty without producing inequalities or choose equality without sacrificing liberty. In any event choice was superfluous because the issue would be decided by "the dumb pressure of common men and machines."[21] Perhaps liberalism itself was only a "way-station," an intellectual by-product of a democracy which was only feasible in an outmoded agricultural society. If liberty had turned out to be the shibboleth of plutocrats, then equality might come in on the wave of the future as an intellectual rationalization of a complex, industrialized world, moving inevitably and impersonally toward a condition of static equilibrium. With a growing sense of futility he told a friend that he had voted for the socialist Norman Thomas because he could not be elected: "I wouldn't want to be in any way responsible for the people that run things at Washington."[22]

As a relativist Becker could not make any more extravagant claims for liberalism than he could for any historian's version of past history. If the historian's task was to be the keeper of the "useful myths" for Mr. Everyman, then, similarly, the political philosopher had to recognize that liberalism and communism were both "useful social myths" based on "emotionally held preconceptions" which determined the choice of the facts that appeared to support them.[23] Instead of saying with Jefferson that "we hold these truths to be self-evident," Becker could only say that these glittering generalities of liberal democracy were useful myths. The confidence of the 18th-century philosophers had rested on the false premises that men are rational devotees of truth and that free speech or discussion inevi-

21. "Liberalism—A Way Station," ibid., p. 98.

22. Letter to William E. Dodd, November 29, 1932, Becker Papers. Curiously enough, in a later reference he implied that he might have voted for Roosevelt in 1932, though he was not sure. See "The Marxian Philosophy of History," in *Everyman His Own Historian*, p. 130.

23. Becker, "New Liberties for Old," in *New Liberties for Old* (New Haven, Yale University Press, 1941), p. 9.

tably promotes the truth and the reconciliation of conflicting interests and opinions, as if modern society could be represented in "a
picture of two amiable, elderly gentlemen engaged in a rational
discussion of the existence of the Deity."[24] Reason was, after all,
from the pragmatic point of view, only "a function of the animal
organism, and truth no more than the perception of discordant experience pragmatically adjusted for a particular purpose and for
the time being."[25] In a scientific world constitutions could not,
like 18th-century ones, draw inspiration from principles, but only
from statistical tables. The modern mind could wax optimistic only
by foreseeing the distant day when "the matter-of-fact apprehension
of experience" would be so greatly extended that the effective
social ideology would take on "the flexible, pragmatic character of
a scientific hypothesis."[26]

Although Becker felt that his common ground with the *philosophes*
of the 18th century had slipped away beneath his feet, he still could
not abandon Condorcet's project, summed up in the title of the
Frenchman's famous work, *Outlines of an Historical View of the
Progress of the Human Mind*. Leo Gershoy has pointed out that Becker
urged modern man "to cut hopes down to size" in order that he
might "edit for twentieth-century expectations" the hopeful Tenth
Epoch of Condorcet's famous tableaux of the stages of Progress.[27]
For Becker the real hope of betterment could no longer be based
on a humanitarian sense of brotherhood or the extension of re-
publicanism; the Heavenly City of the 18th-century philosophers
needed a new foundation built on technology and social science.
If the terrible events of modern history destroyed the comfortable
illusion that the temporal process was getting better and better
through the beneficent influence of "a power not ourselves that
makes for righteousness," he was convinced that an objective

24. "Freedom of Speech," in *Everyman His Own Historian*, p. 104.
25. "Afterthoughts on Constitutions," in *New Liberties for Old*, p. 93.
26. "New Liberties for Old," ibid., p. 43.
27. "Carl Becker on Progress and Power," *AHR*, 55 (1949), 33.

standard for measuring progress could be found by taking an Olympian view of man's development of instruments for the control of nature from the stone flint of the ape-man to the electric eye in the Pennsylvania Station. If he had become disenchanted with the speculative Reason of the Enlightenment, it was only because he was so thoroughly enchanted with the promise of technical Reason, embodied in scientific technology. Reason drunk speculated on moral and political principles; Reason sober pragmatically adjusted itself to circumstances, advanced tentative hypotheses, and built tools to master the environment. The lectures he gave in 1935 at Stanford University, "Progress and Power," were Becker's appeal from Reason drunk to Reason sober.

In this technocratic perspective invention was the mother of necessity, and history could be periodized into major phases by the discoveries of fire, writing, and magnetic force. Through these stages man advanced from farming and hunting to politics, to religion, and to science. Only in the fourth phase, inaugurating the shift from the manipulation of verbal symbols and ideas, which had characterized the previous phase, to absorption in the control of external things with the aid of mathematical science, had progress become systematically possible through the extension of "matter-of-fact knowledge and matter-of-fact apprehension to an ever widening realm of experience."[28] The inner poise based on harmony with one's environment, which primitive man had achieved by seeing the outer world as an extension of himself, could be regained by scientific man, who saw his own personality as merely an integral extension of the outer world of things.[29] In the far distant future, no doubt, new sources of power would finally be exhausted and man would face a stable world. Progress would then be unnecessary because its purpose would have been fulfilled. History was heading toward a "stabilized and scientifically adjusted society" in which man's ideas and habits would be harmoniously accommo-

28. *Progress and Power*, p. 96.
29. Ibid., p. 60.

dated to the matter-of-fact knowledge he had accumulated about himself and his world.[30]

For all his scorn of the impersonality of the scientific historians, Becker's theory of progress was remarkably reminiscent of Henry Adams' periodization of the past in terms of stages of energy. For all his contempt for the positivists with their cult of "cold, hard facts," Becker believed that history, in the long run, "gives its validation to matter-of-fact knowledge while dismissing value judg-ments as useless or insufficiently discriminated."[31] For all his estrangement from the optimistic rationalism of the Enlightenment, he propounded a technocratic dream of a finally adjusted society. O brave new world that has such reason in it! But a 20th-century Miranda might well hesitate to clap her hands in joy at this vision of a bleakly vague and static utopia which fulfills historical progress only at the price of terminating it forever. Yet it was this abstract goal which he was compelled to invoke in order to wrest some gleam of hope from the process of technological change. Technology is the most convenient place to look for evidence of man's increase in power, but Becker was too sophisticated to think that technical progress was an unambiguous guarantee of general human amelio-ration. He was well aware that rapid multiplication of the instru-ments of power greatly increased the tempo and complexity of social change, making ever more glaring the radical discord be-tween man's capacity to control Nature and his ability to subdue society by similar means to rational order. He had begun his specu-lation on progress, in fact, with the warning that one could not talk about it as a movement toward some known good end without having some doctrinal infallibility which he did not claim to possess. But he could not, any more than the *philosophes,* resist the tempta-tion to find in the doctrine of progress the securities that religious dogma had once provided. He therefore dreamed of a day when the same matter-of-fact spirit that inspired scientific technology

30. Ibid., p. 98.
31. Ibid., p. 97.

would control man's thinking about society and he could then make a final adjustment to his world.

Yet what could this formless goal be but a pernicious abstraction? Adjustment to the environment prescribes no particular purposes or values, and the ultimately stabilized society would constitute either a lifeless inertia or a tyranny in which the scientific élite executed its own plans under the pretense of applied engineering. If Becker gave his loyalty to the coming society of statically adjusted forces, he could have no assurance that the process of stabilization would protect the humane and liberal values he fundamentally believed in; they might well be eliminated as mere value judgments "insufficiently discriminated." The glad tidings of the future then being chanted by fascists and communists had little music in them to please the ear of any liberal. The scientist, in putting Nature on trial, could calmly await the results of his tentative hypotheses; but Becker was in the midst of history, himself on trial, the stakes too high for indefinite tentativeness.

Whatever his qualms, he was still enough of a liberal democrat to recognize the menace of the new totalitarianism. Though he was ignorantly and irresponsibly attacked in 1935 by a textbook censorship committee in Washington, D.C., for being a "well-known communistic writer," he declared in that same year in an essay on the Marxian philosophy of history: "I have no faith in the possibility of abolishing oppression by oppressing oppressors. I have no faith in the infallibility of any man, or of any group of men, or of the doctrines or dogmas of any man or group of men, except in so far as they can stand the test of free criticism and analysis." He did not think the dictatorship of a Stalin, a Mussolini, or a Hitler became "something new and admirable by being dressed up in a new and mystical ideology."[32] If it was possible that modern civilization

32. "The Marxian Philosophy of History," in *Everyman His Own Historian*, pp. 125–6. He replied to the charge of being a Communist in a letter to the editor of the Washington *Herald*, November 26, 1935, Becker Papers. Defending his textbook, *Modern History*, he was involved in the irony (for a relativist) of affirming that "the function of the historian is to tell us as accurately as he can what happened."

might fail to find through the means of liberal democracy a cure for the social evils that bred fascism and communism and thus collapse into dictatorship, he steadfastly refused to recognize such an outcome as intrinsically desirable or to join in any effort to make it inevitable. As the new authoritarian systems gained power, the spine of Becker's liberalism began to stiffen. In April 1938 he had scoffed at the danger of the outbreak of a European war; a year and a half later he condemned Hitlerism as a fatal menace to any democratic and humane civilization, which could not be preserved by submitting to the limitless demands and brutalities of Nazi policy.[33]

The challenge of the threat of fascism forced Becker to modify the whole tenor and emphasis of his pragmatic relativism. It seemed to him in 1940 to have reached "a final fantastic form" in the systematic violence and anti-intellectualism of European dictatorships. Truth and morality were made "relative to the purposes of any egocentric somnambulist who can succeed, by a ruthless projection of his personality, in creating the power to impose his unrestrained will upon the world."[34] This totalitarian nightmare was certainly not what Becker meant by pragmatic accommodation to circumstances! If reason was limited, it was not so bankrupt that it could not oppose such hyperbolic pretensions as these. Even if reason was only an instrument of the organism, reason still had to determine the best interest of the organism; even if truth was relative, in some sense, error had to be distinguished and reduced. There were, after all, "some generalities that still glitter": the values of democracy, respect for the dignity of the individual, for persuasion, for the common good, and for the disinterested pursuit of truth, had "a life of their own apart from any particular social system or type of civilization."[35] They were the values which, being celebrated by all

33. "How to Keep Out of War: A Symposium," *Nation,* *146* (1938); 378; "Why Europe Fights," *Cornell Alumni News, 42* (October 12, 1939), *33*.
34. "Some Generalities That Still Glitter," in *New Liberties for Old,* p. 145.
35. Ibid., p. 149.

the saints and sages of the world, readily lent themselves to rational justification, but did not need it. In 1922 he had thought it irrelevant to ask if the ideas of the Declaration of Independence had any validity; twenty years later he affirmed that the phrases of the Declaration, glittering or not, denoted "the fundamental realities that men will always fight for rather than surrender."[36]

Written during the war years, Becker's last two books—*Freedom and Responsibility in the American Way of Life* and *How New Will the Better World Be?*—reflect the confidence of a man who has signed his peace with modern liberal democracy, terminating a long lover's quarrel. He even discovered in the two-party system, with its compromises, vague platforms, and nearly indistinguishable candidates, a conserving, unifying force which softened class and sectional animosities. It was true, he admitted, that the ideals of democracy were not fully lived up to in the United States, but ideals, though imperfectly realized, still measured the aspirations of a people. Trying to prevent the frustration of unreasonable expectations that had precipitated his own disillusionment with Wilson, he deflated the reformer's invidious rhetorical use of the catch phrases of nationalism, power politics, imperialism, and the status quo. Nationalism, expressing modern man's sense of community, was largely responsible for giving most men the impetus to fight the barbarism of the Axis countries; all politics was concerned with power; all the major powers had interests beyond their borders and peace could not be built upon the neglect of them; and if men naturally wished to defend their familiar ways of life, the status quo in the free societies included the basic rights which justified the fight for its preservation. In these sober terms he shored up a democratic faith that had badly sagged in the years between the wars.[37]

36. *The Declaration of Independence* (New York, 1942), p. xvi. Cf. ibid. (1922), p. 278.

37. *Freedom and Responsibility in the American Way of Life* (New York, Knopf, 1945), pp. 84, 105; *How New Will the Better World Be? A Discussion of Post-war Reconstruction* (New York, Knopf, 1944), pp. 74, 83–4, 106–7, 128.

Because he had himself been a part of the malaise he diagnosed, he could indict his generation without self-righteousness. Proud of its sophistication, his generation had been determined on no account to be "taken in." But it had been taken in by the "hard-boiled" realism which failed to appreciate the fundamental merits of democratic institutions; most ironically of all, it had been taken in by its very fear of being taken in. Convinced that science had discovered the whole truth about the world and had solved the mysteries of human behavior, the modern mind believed that reason reported the universe to be void of intelligence and order. Then "the astonishing conclusion was somehow reached that an age which regarded every belief as open to doubt had at last got the low-down on men and things."[38] Lacking any sense of certainty or any vital faith, men took refuge in cynicism, indifference, and flight from the history they did not understand. Becker had not only gone down the same dark road with his generation; he had returned to draw a map of its detours and dead ends. His crisis dramatized in the strains of his own mind the impotence of pragmatic relativism as a basis for liberalism and the weakness of his technocratic rationalism as a guide to history.

It is striking, in retrospect, how clearly Becker's trial of faith betrayed his deep affinity for the 18th century. Like Diderot, as Becker described him, his mind was "far too plastic, too continuously generative and creative, to formulate a rigidly consistent, a perfectly integrated explanation of things; far too curious and inquiring, having formulated such an explanation, to surrender to it past escape."[39] Like Diderot, too, there was in the mind of this 20th-century *philosophe* a conflict between his political liberalism and his metaphysical skepticism. How could Diderot, who longed to be a man of virtue, preach morality when Reason's speculation led to a deterministic materialism in which the will was nothing but

38. "What We Didn't Know Hurt Us a Lot," p. 391.
39. "The Dilemma of Diderot," in *Everyman His Own Historian*, p. 273.

the flickering impulse of desire and aversion? The empirical method, bringing all values to the relative test, was an effective instrument for undermining the theoretical foundations of the *ancien régime*, but if followed through to its conclusion the identification of man with nature meant that all the evils of society were inevitable products of a natural order: "The overturning which men like Diderot dreamed of required some fixed and sure fulcrum not to be found in the shifting sands of relative utility."[40] Yet Diderot's dilemma was also Becker's because he believed that "for good or ill we must regard the world as a continuous flux, a ceaseless and infinitely complicated process of waste and repair, so that 'all things and principles of things' are to be regarded as no more than 'inconstant modes or fashions,' as the 'concurrence, renewed from moment to moment, of forces parting sooner or later on their way.' "[41] From this point of view Becker could find no foothold in the stream of events by which he could get firm control of history, whether as knowledge or as action.

When all issues are regarded as pragmatic ones, involving the particular needs of an organism facing a discordant experience, then order remains elusive. Isolated desires and impulses invoke no systematic order and define no responsibilities. The animus of antiformalism led Becker to devalue principles and institutional forms. But until men reflect on their needs and impulses to weave about their life a fabric of ideals and institutions, they do not emerge from their environment, material or psychological, into the self-conscious life of history. Until life is given a particular focus beyond impulse there are no imperatives, only desires; no history, only happenings. Becker's theory of progress was an attempt to solve a problem he had rendered insoluble by his definition of it: to look for values in a world made meaningful only through facts. Generalizing the bleak implications of the scientific view of the cosmos, the historian who

40. Ibid., p. 281.
41. *The Heavenly City of the Eighteenth-century Philosophers,* p. 12.

had tried to emancipate the study of history from the tyranny of the idol of the laboratory had been in deeper bondage than he knew to the same icon.

Though Becker made a stir among historians by attacking the idea of detached objectivity, his difficulties in meeting the events of his time were intimately rooted in his personal detachment from history. He had said of Henry Adams' autobiography that it was "the story of a man who regarded life from the outside, as a spectator at the play," and he had remarked of Benjamin Franklin that in all of his dealings with men and affairs he was never "wholly committed," Nature alone meeting him with "a disinterestedness matching his own."[42] Surely there is in part a touch of self-portrayal here. Like Adams, Becker seemed at times a spectator of his life in history; like Franklin, never wholly committed, speculation alone absorbing his mind. It was as if Becker had reversed the proper places of partisanship and detachment, linking the former to thought and the latter to action. By dissolving the mind into the context of practical action, he had distorted the role of historical knowledge; by detaching the will from historical institutions and ideals, he had inhibited action. For Becker man was less defined by his attachment to a concrete world of social institutions than he was by his intellect: "Thought makes the whole dignity of man," he quoted Pascal; "therefore endeavor to think well, that is the only morality."[43]

This intellectualist strain justifies the judgment of Leo Gershoy that "the transplanted Iowa farm boy did not venture far from his spiritual home in Adam Smith's Edinburgh or the Paris of the *philosophes*."[44] Becker's final conclusion that the values he cherished were the common stock of the saints and sages of the past two thousand or more years was in keeping with the eclectic deism of

42. "The Education of Henry Adams," in *Everyman His Own Historian,* p. 147; "Benjamin Franklin," *Dictionary of American Biography, 6* (1943), 597.
43. Used as a motto for Becker, *Modern Democracy,* New Haven, Yale University Press, 1941.
44. "Carl Becker on Progress and Power," *AHR, 55* (1949), 31.

the 18th-century rationalists who believed they had found the common core of all religions. It was an odd conclusion for a modern historian to make, for what could this ideal consensus of all the wise men be but a pale abstraction from the complex and conflicting currents of history, soaring at last beyond history altogether into the realm of essence? Yet this return to the faith of the Enlightenment seemed to him to be the only alternative to a pragmatism which had culminated in a sterile technocratic dream of a scientifically adjusted society. The terms of his choice obscured the very nature of historical reality, which has its being neither in man's power over the external environment nor in his communion with eternal self-evident truths, but rather in the creative efforts of his will to organize his finite values in the concrete world of institutions. History's conflicts cannot be composed by technology or intellect, however skilled, but only by the will that engenders and suffers them. In the light of the cruel severity of history, which demands absolute decisions from men who live in a relative, limited situation, Becker's intellectual charm, the bitter-sweet mood of a disenchanted urbanity, has a certain fragility.

It was, indeed, the Heavenly City that fascinated him. Even in his studies of revolution he betrayed, as George H. Sabine has pointed out, "a preference for the cool ardors of the philosophers who preceded a revolution and his distrust of the violent emotions without which revolutions cannot be made."[45] Fate compelled him to live in a time of revolutions, as Sabine noted, for which neither Thomas Jefferson nor John Dewey were appropriate symbols. Becker had, at least, that creative plasticity of mind he admired in Diderot. It kept him, as well as Diderot, from surrendering to his skepticism past escape: "If Stalin and Hitler have taught me something, so much the better."[46] If he had had fewer doubts, he might never have had any problems worth mentioning, nor would he

45. Sabine, Intro. to *Freedom and Responsibility in the American Way of Life,* p. xxxi.

46. Becker, Intro. to *New Liberties for Old,* p. xvi.

have left behind him when he died, on April 10, 1945, a body of work which stands as a record of a liberal mind, made piquant and profound by the probings of a resilient spirit. Inheriting the dilemmas of the Enlightenment, he had acquired its virtues: the wry wit of a Franklin, the civilized felicity of a Jefferson, the humane reasonableness of a Diderot.

CHAPTER SEVEN

The Devil's Adversary

CHARLES BEARD's reputation was born in controversy, and it was characteristic that on his death he left historians a legacy of bitter dispute about his last two books. Though they were as provocative of passion as his study of the Constitution, the scandalized and the delighted had, for the most part, changed roles this time. Whereas in 1913 the conservatives had been horrified at what they thought was Beard's muckraking of the Constitution and its framers, while the reformers had concluded that Beard had shown American government to be ripe for change, thirty-five years later the conservatives hailed Beard as an ally and the liberals lamented his woeful fall from grace. The fundamental changes had taken place, however, not so much in Beard as in history; as always he maintained his independence. Those reactionary members of the America First Committee who found oil to feed their fires of hatred in Beard's indictment of President Roosevelt's foreign policy were far more widely separated from his spirit than even the socialist and progressive reformers had been in the period before the first World War. The practical categories of the political world are not complex enough to contain his mind; when they are applied to it, his point of view escapes them. Like Becker, Beard must be seen as a philosophical historian trying to pick his way through the tangled jungle of the modern world.

The impact of two world wars on Beard, as on Becker, produced a troubled search for intellectual orientation; like Becker, Beard also constructed a theory of progress as an ally of liberalism; and for him, too, the pragmatic revolt against scientific history played a crucial role in defining the course and character of his inner conflicts. Yet the temperamental difference between the two men was reflected in their peculiar difficulties. Whereas Becker's crisis of confidence was largely ideological, rooted in his skepticism and his impersonal approach to the idea of progress, Beard's anxieties pivoted around the practical issue of American foreign policy and were sharpened by the very ardor of his attachment to the goals of his idealistic conception of the promise of American life. Becker's revision of relativism coincided with his defense of democracy against fascism, even if this meant going to war; Beard's revision of economic determinism, under the influence of relativism, strengthened his determination to defend the cause of isolationism, even if this meant a scathing denunciation of Roosevelt's interventionist policy.

Though Beard was an isolationist, he cannot be dismissed as one of those whose xenophobia and complacency made them proponents of "America First" in a world at war. "The conception of America as a self-constituted, hermit-kingdom," he wrote in 1935, "is false to facts and the scorn that many Americans pour on the Old World is an evidence of infantilism, not of strength."[1] Yet that same year he made a plea for America to withdraw from "the hateful conflicts of passionate acquisition in Europe and the Orient" and offer to the world "the strange sight of a national garden well tended."[2] Six years later his name was among those who signed a roster, publicized by General Wood of the America First Committee, condemning President Roosevelt's "shoot-on-sight" order to Atlantic patrols.[3] The forces that made Beard an isolationist—a term he disliked, preferring to call himself a "continentalist"—

1. "That Promise of American Life," *New Republic*, 81 (1935), 350.

2. *The Open Door at Home: A Trial Philosophy of National Interest*, p. 319.

3. Wayne S. Cole, *America First: The Battle against Intervention* (Madison, University of Wisconsin Press, 1953), p. 161. Beard signed the statement as an independent sympathizer, not as a member of "America First."

were deeply rooted in the fundamental texture of his historical thinking.

In his last book Beard noted that "what had happened as a result of opening up diplomatic archives after World War I seemed to forecast probable lines of historical investigation during the next twenty-five or fifty years."[4] The full force of his recoil from American intervention in 1917 was, however, long delayed. When it came at last, the spring snapped all the more powerfully for the accumulated tension of over twenty-five years of anxious reassessment of American policy. When war came in 1917 he vigorously supported Wilson, convinced that the German military machine represented a brutal conspiracy against democracy and threatened all mankind, while Wilson's principles for a new world order heralded "the opening of a new epoch in the rise of government by the people and in the growth of a concert among the nations"—an era which would be as momentous as that of the American and French Revolutions.[5] When Beard resigned from Columbia University in the fall of 1917 in protest against the dropping of three teachers for their opposition to the war, it was not because he had any sympathy for their opinions. He had himself been grilled by suspicious trustees because of his outspoken defense of freedom of speech, and he believed a small group of them were determined "to humiliate or terrorize every man who held progressive, liberal, or unconventional views in political matters."[6] For him the issue had nothing to do with the merits of intervention in the war; it had to do with whether the university was a center of free inquiry or a mere department store selling standardized goods on demand.

4. *President Roosevelt and the Coming of the War, 1941: A Study in Appearances and Realities* (New Haven, Yale University Press, 1948), p. 234, n. 1.

5. Beard and Frederick A. Ogg, *National Governments and the World War* (New York, Macmillan, 1919), p. 570; and see also Beard, "A Call upon Every Citizen," *Harper's, 137* (1918), 655.

6. "A Statement by Charles A. Beard," *New Republic, 13* (1917), 250. For his letter of resignation see *School and Society, 6* (1917), 446-7.

After Germany, Austria, and Russia, having nothing to lose, opened up their secret archives, the "revisionist" movement among historians developed, and it took on the proportions of a crusade in the late 1920's. In the books of Harry Elmer Barnes and one of his students, C. Hartley Grattan, the public could read how historians had largely removed the burden of war guilt from the Central Powers to settle it upon the Allies and had explained American intervention by economic, not idealistic, reasons.[7] Beard himself had gone to Europe to examine the new revelations from the diplomatic pouches, and in the pages of the *New Republic,* to which he was a frequent contributor, he could follow the whole story of the diplomatic disclosures and read the serialization of John Maynard Keynes' *The Economic Consequences of the Peace,* a devastating portrayal of the alleged swindling of Wilson by the imperialists at the Peace Conference. Yet it is notable how relatively restrained Beard's reaction was to the findings of the "revisionists." In a series of lectures at Dartmouth, published in 1922 as *Cross Currents in Europe To-day,* he acknowledged the dissolution of official myths about the war, but he still felt that European affairs ran to "the root of our national destiny,"[8] the United States being woven ever more closely into an international economic order. The immediate moral of the opening of the archives was that Europe should set its own house in order under the stress of its own vicissitudes and experiences by forming a European league. Since imperialism had fanned the sparks that ignited the war, then the proper course was to abandon imperialistic policies. America might then, giving up its own empire, forego "the legacy of Caesar" for "the heritage of Athens" and join the League of Nations.[9]

By 1926, having lived through the postwar wave of conformism

7. See Selig Adler, "The War-guilt Question and American Disillusionment, 1918–1928," *Journal of Modern History, 23* (1951), 1–28.

8. *Cross Currents in Europe To-day* (Boston, Marshall Jones, 1922), p. 1.

9. Ibid., pp. 269–71.

and intolerance, he had serious doubts whether constitutional government could be maintained in the throes of another great war, but he still did not look upon American intervention in 1917 as a ruinous mistake. Americans had been right to fear for the fate of democracy. Anyone not obsessed by pacificism or German sympathies (and Beard was free of both) had to admit, he believed, that a triumphant German military party would soon have challenged Washington. Americans were well advised, therefore, to prevent the rise of any single European power to a dominant position and to look on European quarrels with cold blood only to calculate the balance of power all the more effectively. "Merely to shift heroes and villains," he reminded his "revisionist" friend and former colleague Barnes, "will only confuse the issue."[10] Though the second volume of Beard's *The Rise of American Civilization* stressed the excesses of the war passion in America and noted the grimy aspects of its diplomatic background, he still felt that, despite propaganda and economic pressures, the German submarine campaign and the balance of power were vital factors in producing American intervention.[11] As the 20's ended, he faced the future with confidence. Only a few months before the stock-market crash and the ensuing worldwide depression, he put his hope in the development of international capitalism as "the best pledge of peace" in a world of declining feudalism, plagued by fanatical nationalism and revolutionary communism. Businessmen would much prefer the profits of peace to the passions of war. Despite its "myth of isolation," the United States was by its economic power an influential if unofficial member of the League of Nations. Because American credit had carried the Allies to victory in the war, future aggressors would, he

10. "Heroes and Villains of the World War," *Current History, 24* (1926), 735. For his concern about the impact of war on constitutional government see "The Great American Tradition," *Nation, 123* (1926), 7–8.

11. *The Rise of American Civilization* (rev. college ed. New York, 1934), *2*, 630–1.

felt, be given pause by the "almost dead certainty" that the United
States would again "throw her sword into the scales."[12]

Not, at this point, either an orthodox "revisionist" or an isolationist, Beard was to become in the next decade a leading intellectual
spokesman for the anti-interventionist cause, and when the crisis
of war approached he was doing all he could to oppose the "almost
dead certainty" of American participation in world conflict.
"Master publicists are made largely by time and circumstance," he
once wrote; "and it is given to few men to write the moral philosophy for the political passion of a great age, or to clothe a powerful social interest in the form of an inexorable and compelling
logic."[13] Though written in 1910, this statement, if applied to Beard
after 1934, becomes an unconsciously prophetic self-portrayal.
What had happened to bring him to this conclusion was the stunning
impact on his mind of the severe shock of the Depression, the vivid
hope of recovery and reform through national planning under the
New Deal, and the sensational Congressional investigations into the
economic background of American diplomacy. These events acted
as a powerful catalyst to crystallize his basic ideas into a new and
fixed form.

The depression was a challenge, he wrote in 1930, to make a "re-
discovery" of the Founding Fathers by creating a new science of
political economy that would be the *Federalist* of modern times, im-
plemented by statecraft as boldly constructive as that of the Constitutional Convention. The "everlasting battle of capitalism and
agriculture for advantage," which had been the theme of his historical writing, must now be transcended by a program having its
bench marks "not in the bald interests of cotton spinners or wheat

12. "Prospects for Peace," *Harper's, 158* (1929), 320, 327. For his fear that
isolationism might be used to weaken national security see Beard and William
Beard, *The American Leviathan: The Republic in the Machine Age* (New York,
Macmillan, 1930), p. 736.

13. "The Study and Teaching of Politics," *Columbia University Quarterly,
12* (1910), 269.

raisers, but in the very center of Planned National Economy."[14] Beard's work as director of the Training School for Public Service of the New York Bureau for Municipal Research was an expression of his profound interest in the problems of city planning. Widely recognized as an expert, he had offered his talents generously when the Japanese Home Minister called upon him for advice in reconstructing the city of Tokyo after the earthquake of 1923 and when the American Yugoslav Society urged him in 1927 to go to Belgrade to make a study of the government of Yugoslavia.[15] It was inevitable that Beard would see the Depression as an opportunity for the extension of planning to the national level. That idea of progress which he had defended as a young graduate student at Oxford in his first book seemed now to have a magnificent chance for realization: the "masters of the new technology" could at last put reason into society if they would "seize upon, rationalize, and idealize the best elements of their order."[16] Nearly two years before the New Deal he drew up "A 'Five-Year Plan' for America" as a working blueprint for an economically consolidated and centrally planned society.

It is one of the lessons of history, Beard believed, that "when it is dark enough you can see the stars."[17] As a philosopher of progress he was sure he could see them. In *The Open Door at Home* he presented his glimpse of the heavens to a generation that had lost its way. Modern man was caught in a tragic conflict between the ideal

14. "Whom Does Congress Represent?" *Harper's, 160* (1930), 152.

15. For the fruit of these trips see his *The Administration and Politics of Tokyo: A Survey and Opinions* (New York, Macmillan, 1923) and *The Balkan Pivot: Yugoslavia; A Study in Government and Administration,* collab. George Radin (New York, Macmillan, 1929).

16. *Toward Civilization,* ed. Beard (New York, 1930), p. 302. For details of his plan see his "A 'Five-Year Plan' for America," *Forum, 86* (1931), 1–11, and "The World as I Want It," *Forum, 91* (1934), 332–4.

17. So he told George Counts. See the latter's "Charles Beard, the Public Man," *Charles A. Beard: An Appraisal,* ed. Howard K. Beale (Lexington, University of Kentucky Press, 1954), p. 252.

and the real—"between a positive knowledge of the possibility of a good and abundant life, demonstrated by physical science and human industry on the one side, and an equally positive knowledge of the miseries, sufferings, cruelties, and ugliness of the world as it actually exists, on the other."[18] Salvation lay in bending man's will to rationalize history by raising the standard of living through an efficient distribution of wealth and the political control of the processes of production and consumption. If Beard's theory of progress indicated the solution, his philosophy of history as "an act of faith" in the future gave him his warrant. The upshot of his attack upon scientific history was the assertion that the historian was obligated to hitch his wagon to a star, and Beard found his polestar in the conception of a "collectivist democracy" that would, by giving up "the diplomacy of the dollar, the navy, and the marines," teach the world the most effective lesson of all in providing an example of "a national garden well tended."[19]

Like many intelligent men, he was convinced that the possibility of American intervention in the second World War posed a threat to the hope of domestic reform. Wilson's policy had split the reformers in 1917, and his progressivism had been diverted and compromised by the exigencies of war. It was, Beard felt, the reform spirit of 1914, not the war spirit of 1917, that, "clarified and informed by recent history," had "its warrant and its task in 1939."[20] His revised estimate of Wilson's foreign policy was the result of many years of anxious scrutiny, finally precipitated into hostile conclusion by the probe into the munitions industry conducted in 1934 by Senator Gerald P. Nye's committee, climaxing a whole series of investigations into "dollar diplomacy." This melodramatic exposé, which seemed to Beard to be more important than any disclosures since the opening of the European archives, convinced him that "sinister enterprises," conspiring to tie America closer to Britain through credit arrangements, had forced the United States

18. *The Open Door at Home,* p. 16.
19. Ibid., p. 319.
20. "Looking Backward," *New Republic, 101* (1939), 80.

into war in 1917. In his *The Devil Theory of War,* a broadside against the notion that wicked men make war, he concluded that "powerful economic and political personalities," trying to avoid a domestic crisis by extending credits and loans to the Allies, had finally averted a crash "by leading the country into war."[21] Despite the fact that this tract was a skeptical thrust at moralistic or dogmatic historians who wrote as if they knew the cause of great events and could put their fingers on the villains, he, nevertheless, gave his readers the vivid impression that Wilson had succumbed to the insistent pressures of bankers, thus causing American intervention. Beard's initial skepticism only cleared the ground for his dogmatic economic interpretation, and it was with no little moral passion that he later pronounced the judgment that "the cruelty and justice of history" had rent for good the "grand fabric of official imagination" about why America went to war in 1917. If the imperial hopes for empire in 1900 had collapsed, so also had the "philanthropic enthusiasm" of Wilson been irrevocably deflated. "Some new mask," he ominously hinted, "might be needed for the face of war."[22]

If by 1935 Beard had enthusiastically joined the ranks of the first World War "revisionists," he had also at the same time deliberately set the stage for his appearance in 1946 as the leading "revisionist" historian of the second World War. The economic interpretation, always in his hands a prolific source of dualistic thinking, led him to see a historical conflict between Jefferson's continentalism, based on the interests of farmers and planters, and Hamilton's dream of empire, rooted in the interests of merchants, traders, and capitalists. In Roosevelt's policy of economic nationalism and a strong navy, these opposing outlooks seemed to have merged by 1934. The time had come for clarification and enunciation of a new policy by a

---

21. *The Devil Theory of War* (New York, Vanguard, 1936), p. 107. For his reaction to the Nye Committee's work see his "Emerging Issues in America," *Current History, 41* (1934), 203–9, and "On Keeping Out of War," *Current History, 43* (1936), 625–32.

22. Charles A. and Mary R. Beard, *America in Midpassage* (New York, 1939), *1,* 432–3.

statesman as great as Jefferson or Hamilton.[23] Was Roosevelt statesman enough to meet this challenge? Beard agonized over the president's failure to see the issue in these terms. On the one hand, as the architect of the New Deal, who seemed to share Beard's act of faith in collectivist democracy, Roosevelt was one of the greatest Americans, having "penetrated deeper into the aspirations and tragedy of American life than any of their heroes."[24] On the other hand, the President's position on foreign affairs was obscure. Beard trembled when he reflected that Jefferson, Jackson, and Wilson had all suffered their reform programs to be blighted by war. The course of history threatened grimly to repeat itself. Did not Roosevelt have a touch of Wilson's tendency "to seek the delusion of world grandeur"?[25] Would he, too, confronted by the same choice Wilson had faced, indulge his messianic temptation to play a large role in international politics, yield to the pressures of economic interests, unite a divided party, and postpone the defeat of his domestic program by pouring out "American blood and treasure" to "the advantage of British and French imperialism"?[26] Over six years before Pearl Harbor, Beard was already fearfully sure that Roosevelt would go down the same dark path to war. He would not openly plunge the country into war in order to escape an economic crisis; there would be an "incident" or "provocation" easily magnified into a just cause. Beard had defined the great historian as the one who wove the warp of the future into the weft of the past by an act of prophetic discernment, proving his power by the accuracy of his prediction. Taking up the mantle of Cassandra in February 1935, he announced: "The Pacific war awaits."[27]

23. *The Idea of National Interest: An Analytical Study of American Foreign Policy*, collab. G. H. E. Smith (New York, Macmillan, 1934), p. 553. For Becker's review see "A Fine Pair of Words," *Yale Review*, 23 (1934), 814–17.

24. "Roosevelt's Place in History," *Events*, 3 (1938), 86.

25. " 'Going Ahead' with Roosevelt," *Events*, 1 (1937), 12.

26. "Our Choice in Foreign Policy," *Events*, 1 (1937), 164. See also "Those Old-world Quarrels," *Events*, 2 (1937), 262.

27. "National Politics and War," *Scribner's*, 97 (1935), 70.

Thereafter Beard's historical writing became an increasingly tendentious and sardonically phrased plea for a policy of continentalism: "a recognition of the limited nature of American power to relieve, restore, and maintain life beyond its own sphere of interest and control—a recognition of the hard fact that the United States, either alone or in any coalition, did not possess the power to force peace on Europe and Asia, to assure the establishment of democratic and pacific governments there, or to provide the social and economic underwriting necessary to the perdurance of such governments."[28] True to his concept of the historian as statesman without portfolio, he abandoned the scholarly detachment that had long ago kept him from speaking to the New York Bar on the Constitution. He appeared before the House Committee on Naval Affairs to speak against the building up of a big navy; he testified in the Senate Foreign Relations Committee against the Lend Lease program; and he was consulted for advice by such prominent isolationists as Col. Charles A. Lindbergh. In the pages of the *Congressional Record* Beard's testimony and his tract *Giddy Minds and Foreign Quarrels* appeared as weapons in the hands of isolationist senators and representatives, who found potent ammunition for their cause by quoting the passionate urging of one of America's foremost historians that we should "stay out to the last ditch, and preserve one stronghold of order and sanity, even against the gates of hell."[29]

28. *A Foreign Policy for America* (New York, Knopf, 1940), p. 152.

29. Quoted from Beard's testimony before the Senate Foreign Relations Committee by Sen. Capper, *Congressional Record,* 77th Cong., 1st sess., 87:2 (February 22, 1941), 1273. For Beard's full testimony see ibid., 87:10 (February 13, 1941), A625–A627, his remarks being put into the *Record* by Senator Burton K. Wheeler. Beard's "Giddy Minds and Foreign Quarrels" appears in ibid., 87:12 (July 10, 1941), A3351–A3356. He was also quoted by Rep. Blackney in the House, ibid., 76th Cong. 2d sess., 85:1 (October 31, 1939), 1140. For his testimony regarding naval policy see "Statement of Dr. Charles A. Beard, Historian," February 10, 1938, *House Committee on Naval Affairs Hearings on House Resolution 9218,* 75th Cong., 3d sess., 2133–2146. Col. Lindbergh visited Beard at New Milford for support and advice sometime in 1940 or 1941, letter from Lindbergh to author, September 26, 1956.

The last three volumes of the Beards' series, The Rise of American Civilization—*America in Midpassage* (2 vols.) and *The American Spirit*—are vibrant with the sense of crisis and the vision of a unique society whose pursuit of the dream of progress has been menaced by foreign critics, imperialistic adventurers, and acquisitive capitalists. It was no accident that Beard had a special fondness for the closing lines of Shelley's *Prometheus Unbound*.[30] With all of his great talent and personal force he was determined to put his faith in the hope that, in Shelley's phrase, "creates from the wreck of hope the thing it contemplates." Yet his ardor was not strong enough to bend the course of history to his will. When the Japanese attacked Pearl Harbor on December 7, 1941, he knew that he had failed. But at the same time he must have nursed the corrosive confidence that, after all, he had six years before predicted the event. It is against the background of this tense frame of mind that Beard's last two books on Roosevelt's foreign policy must be understood.

In these two volumes Beard wore a mask of frigid impersonality which, though lowered briefly in footnotes or by an insinuating phrase in the first book, was not clearly dropped until the second. In the first, *American Foreign Policy in the Making, 1932–1940: A Study in Responsibilities,* he diligently cited the public record of Roosevelt's protestations of neutrality, peace sentiments, and disavowal of entangling alliances. A reader with nothing else to go on might have concluded that Beard's purpose was to show that the president, in a wavering way, was really an isolationist at heart. But, since the book was published in 1946, readers had the knowledge that America had gone to war finally in close collaboration with the Allies. Even so, many reviewers were puzzled about Beard's aim, but in his eyes the record itself was, given the final results, sufficiently damning.[31] Readers of the next volume, *President*

30. Arthur W. Macmahon, "Charles Austin Beard as a Teacher," *Political Science Quarterly, 65* (1950), 9.

31. Letter to Harry Elmer Barnes, August 7 [no year], Barnes file, about *American Foreign Policy in the Making, 1932–1940*, New Haven, Yale University Press, 1946.

Roosevelt and the Coming of the War, 1941, were left with no doubts. The impersonal tone—managed now, one suspects, only by an effort at self-control—could not diminish the force of the sensational conclusion of his narrative, pointedly subtitled *A Study in Appearances and Realities.* In 1937, discussing the causes of the first World War, Beard had insisted that historians had not yet found a person in authority who made a statement he knew would bring about in the minds of the enemy negotiators a reaction precipitating war.[32] Beard now was sure he could answer such a question about the second World War. Because the war did not come in the Atlantic, where there were many incidents to "exploit" if Roosevelt wanted to bring it about, Beard decided that by November 1, 1941, the president had exhausted his "expedients" in that area.[33] Since the president had told Ambassador Grew in Tokyo that American strategy had to be global, taking advantage of every opportunity on every front to contribute to national security, Beard believed that the high policy was to deliberately maneuver the Japanese into attacking America, a plan conceived "as a phase of assistance to Great Britain in a world of inseparable spheres of interest."[34] The plot was clearly revealed, he felt, in a notation in Secretary of War Stimson's diary. The entry recorded a conference of the president and his top diplomatic and military advisors on November 25, 1941 at which the question had been raised as to how, in view of an imminent secret attack, the enemy might be maneuvered into the position of firing the first shot without allowing too much danger to ourselves.[35] It seemed to Beard as if the gloomy prognostication he had made in 1935 had been verified by events.

Despite his scholarly documentation and Olympian tone, his ar-

---

32. "Why Did We Go to War?" *New Republic,* 90 (1937), 127.
33. *President Roosevelt and the Coming of the War, 1941,* p. 149.
34. Ibid., p. 485.
35. Ibid., p. 517. For a non-invidious explanation of this incident see Herbert Feis, *The Road to Pearl Harbor: The Coming of the War between the United States and Japan* (Princeton, Princeton University Press, 1950), pp. 314–15.

gument was, in substance, highly sensational: the president, in
collaboration with his lieutenants, had by means of a deep-dyed
deception put the Republic in jeopardy by secretly scrapping traditional isolationist policy even at the cost of the lives and reputations
of the Pearl Harbor base's personnel, whose leaders he had later made
sacrificial victims on the high altar of his schemes. The Chicago
Daily Tribune grasped the sinister implications of the charge in an
editorial, "The Tangled Web," written for its own extreme right-
wing purposes, asserting that Beard had shown the president and
"his stooges" to be the greatest enemies of the Republic known to
history.[36] In this hyperbolic reaction Beard's last works found an
echo, a reverberation that jangles harshly, like a raucous bell tolling
the bitter end of one of the most remarkable careers in American
intellectual life.

His thesis was not the first such charge, nor has it been the last.
Though there are soberly documented histories that have since been
written which give no support whatever to the "revisionist" case,
a "revisionist" school still flourishes.[37] For all its accusatory temper
it is now on the defensive, exhibiting many of the strident signs of
any minority group that feels it has not been taken seriously enough.
Conflicting historical interpretations of great wars are endemic, and
a charge similar to the one directed at Roosevelt has been made by
some modern scholars, for example, against Lincoln's handling of
the crisis of Fort Sumter. Yet whatever the merits of the specific
arguments in these cases may be, it is evident that Beard's narrative
stemmed directly from his passionate prior conviction that Roosevelt was mistaken in his policy, deceitful in his defense of it, and

36. April 5, 1948, p. 18.
37. For representative arguments of the "revisionists" see Harry Elmer
Barnes, ed., *Perpetual War for Perpetual Peace*, Caldwell, Idaho, Caxton, 1953.
For cogent criticism of the "revisionists" see Herbert Feis, "War Came at
Pearl Harbor: Suspicions Considered," *Yale Review, 45* (1956), 378–90, and
Robert H. Ferrell, "Pearl Harbor and the Revisionists," *Historian, 17* (1955),
215–33.

irresponsible in his execution of it. With all his prodigious power of scholarly analysis and assault Beard was trying by means of written history to enter a caustic protest against the course of actual events.

His last pages were written in a mood of despair. Russia, helped by American aid and by Allied defeat of Germany, had risen as a formidable antagonist to the free world. Americans, more than ever committed to spending money, material, and men on military service, faced an uncertain future, the victims of an international situation in which they were involved, but which they could not control. Under the pressure of new domestic issues the hope of a vigorous reform party had disappeared, and the presidency had become dangerously swollen in scope and power. The future for representative government was, Beard judged, utterly bleak.[38] To such grim results, he implied, had Roosevelt's policy brought us!

The "revisionists," especially Beard's friend Barnes, have made much of the danger of having recent history told by "court historians," too closely connected with the administration to be independent, impartial scholars. But the wisdom in this warning is not sufficient to establish Beard's status as a free investigator. Scornfully free of any administration commitments, he was, nevertheless, ardently and intimately engaged with the opposition to the administration. Much of his evidence for his last two books came, in fact, from the results of the investigation into Pearl Harbor by a Senate committee with whom he had worked as an adviser.[39] Doubtless every historian of this phase of American diplomacy felt concern as a private citizen for its outcome; but it is unlikely that anyone else had so deliberately and intensely prejudged the record as early as February 1935. One can be sure that Beard himself would have been most suspicious of, say, a history of Jefferson's administration written by an ardent supporter of Alexander Hamilton.

38. *President Roosevelt and the Coming of the War, 1941*, p. 581.
39. George R. Leighton, "Beard and Foreign Policy," in *Charles A. Beard: An Appraisal*, p. 183. Beard's son-in-law, Alfred Vagts, confirmed this fact in an interview.

If other historians have come to different conclusions from reading the evidence Beard cited, it is largely because his frame of
reference gave to that evidence a sinister import. The administration
had chosen, for political reasons, to emphasize to the American
people the risks of what might happen if support were not given to
the Allies, instead of stressing the risks of what might happen if
policies of support were pursued. This tactic had the disadvantage,
of course, as Herbert Feis has pointed out, of leaving the president
"open to a charge of blunder or bad faith if the United States found
itself at war."[40] It was into that opening that Beard stepped. For
him the very fact that war had come seemed to "prove" (by a
post hoc ergo propter hoc fallacy) that "the explanation and promises"
made to the effect that Lend Lease was not a declaration of war had
been "intentionally deceptive."[41] Beard's conceptual categories
were once again Manichaean: extreme isolationism or extreme internationalism. These guiding abstractions, set forth at the beginning
of his narrative, left no room for a middle course of limited internationalism which, while avoiding entangling alliances or prior
commitments, would foster methods of exchange, conference, and
parallel action with countries having common interests and purposes.[42] Thus he made the gap between Roosevelt's public statements and his practical policy appear to be much wider than it
really was, and his narrative took on the journalistic cast of a "scoop"
exposing the sordid realities behind the façade of appearances.

It is striking, as Max Lerner has remarked, how Beard's economic
interpretation constantly led him to a conspiratorial theory of his-

40. *The Road to Pearl Harbor*, p. 134.

41. *President Roosevelt and the Coming of the War, 1941*, p. 154.

42. This point is the basis of Basil Rauch's refutation of Beard's account
through a detailed history of this policy of limited internationalism in *Roosevelt
from Munich to Pearl Harbor: A Study in the Creation of a Foreign Policy*, New
York, Creative Age, 1950. Unfortunately Rauch attacks Beard's devil-theory
of Roosevelt at the price of creating a devil-theory of Beard by accusing him
of deliberate falsification of the record.

tory.[43] If there are always "real" economic reasons lurking behind the individual's ideal "apparent" reasons, then history teems with conspiracies. Thus he was quick to sniff the odor of imperialism on every tainted breeze, and he saw the Japanese attack on Pearl Harbor as the bitter fruit of a hundred years of America's expansionist diplomacy in the Far East. His animus fixed on the fact that Roose-velt had had an ancestor in the China trade and had been Assistant Secretary of the Navy when operations in Mexico, Santo Domingo, and Haiti were being carried on "in the classical imperialist style."[44] Beard was in this way powerfully drawn to the "Devil Theory of War" he had once attacked. He began his study of Roosevelt's policy with sharp criticism of those historians who were so un-sophisticated that they put the blame for the second World War on the wicked propensities of isolationists like Senator Lodge, his cohorts in the Senate, the American public, or even President Wilson for his stubborn refusal of amendments to the Treaty, thus ensuring rejection of the League of Nations by the Senate. Causes in history could not, Beard argued plausibly, be so simply and moralistically ascertained. Japan, Italy, and Germany had, after all, "direct and great relevance" to the coming of the war in Europe.[45] These preliminaries hardly prepared the reader for what was to follow. He then went on to propound an even simpler version of history which featured the villainy of the wicked Roosevelt and his unscrupulous entourage. The devils Beard failed to exorcize came back to plague him with a vengeance! Under their influence he forgot his own earlier criticism of the "revisionists" of the first World War who merely shifted heroes and villains about under the guise of historical analysis.

43. "Beard's 'Economic Interpretation of the Constitution,' " in *Books That Changed Our Minds: A Symposium,* ed. Malcolm Cowley and Bernard Smith (New York, 1939), p. 160.

44. *American Foreign Policy in the Making, 1932–1940,* p. 143; and cf. *President Roosevelt and the Coming of the War, 1941,* p. 234, n. 1.

45. *American Foreign Policy in the Making, 1932–1940,* pp. 40–2.

In 1917 Beard's toughmindedness had led him to point out that diplomacy "calls for poise, cold-bloodedness, and a Machiavellian disposition to see things as they are and to deal with them as they are—whether we like them or not." With equal cogency he added: "A painful consciousness of the rectitude of our intentions and the purity of our purposes is more likely to be a nuisance than a service."[46] Twenty years later he could still grudgingly admit that it was reasonable to ask if peace would be possible "with Hitler and Goering, backed by Mussolini, in possession of the Atlantic trident."[47] Yet he seemed much more concerned with the imperfections of our allies and the dangers of repeating the alleged mistakes of our entrance into the first World War than he was with any realistic calculation of the balance of power. As enemy aggression expanded, he, like so many others, seemed to be hypnotized by the first World War, as if passing legislation which might have kept us out of that war was an adequate response to the problems posed by the second World War. There were many supporters of Roosevelt's foreign policy who felt that not Beard but Carl Becker was now the realist when he wrote in October 1939: "It will be said that a humane and democratic civilization can neither be propagated nor preserved by means of war. It will be said that the last war was fought to make the world safe for democracy and ended by making half of Europe safe for dictators. That is true. But while war can do nothing to safeguard democratic institutions, it may be the only means of preserving the power and independence of democratic countries."[48]

There was always, of course, a tender-minded, idealistic other side to Beard's tough-minded realism. As a philosopher of progress and a man who had made an act of faith in an isolated, collectivist democracy, he had himself something of that "painful consciousness" of the rectitude of his intentions and of the purity of his

46. "A Communication: Perils of Diplomacy," *New Republic, 11* (1917), 136.

47. "America's 'Duty' to England," *Events, 2* (1937), 327.

48. Becker, "Why Europe Fights," *Cornell Alumni News, 42* (1939), 33.

purposes, but he had it on behalf of his beloved American Republic, perpetually endangered by the contamination of European history "encrusted in the blood-rust of fifty centuries."[49] His commitment to this moving, if utopian, dream illustrates the truth of K. R. Popper's remark that for utopians the conspiratorial theory of history has special appeal because "the only explanation of their failure to produce their heaven [is] the evil intentions of the devil who has a vested interest in hell."[50] His last works, which read like counter-plots against the arch-plotter Roosevelt, have the consistency of a man who believed that the historian should draw the outlines of the past in terms of an active faith in the future. With what a sense of outraged sanity must Beard have watched history move not toward his predicted and cherished goal of a last outpost of collectivist democracy, where men reaped the harvests of an abundant civilization, blessed by technological triumph, but instead toward American intervention in a vast war. It could not be, he must have felt, that history had announced there was to be no last refuge "even against the gates of hell." Some perverse interference must have deflected the proper course of history. Beard's act of faith was a bold toss of the dice; the stakes were too high for him to lose gracefully. Some-one must have rigged the game. There had, therefore, to be some villainous dark soul who had arrogantly upset the best laid plans of thinking men. In his indictment of Roosevelt all the various threads of Beard's historical philosophy came together with as impressive an appearance of inexorability as could be found in his own accounts of the remorseless sweep of historical forces.

To those who do not share his "act of faith" Beard seems to have been blinded by the radiance of his own ideals to the issue of American security in a world menaced by totalitarian aggression. It seemed to him, on the contrary, that the "world-savers," as he contemptuously called them, were the ones who would ruin the Re-

49. "Collective Security: A Debate," *New Republic, 93* (1938), 359.
50. *The Open Society and Its Enemies* (rev. ed., Princeton, Princeton University Press, 1950), p. 288.

public for the sake of their schemes.[51] There was an element of hard wisdom in Beard's belief that American power was not omnipotent, that it could not reshape Europe to its heart's desire, or assume total responsibility for what happened everywhere. On the interventionist side there were not a few idealists who were as utopian in their dreams of world planning as Beard ever was in his vision of national planning. Whatever disagreement one has with his final position on foreign affairs, one cannot help responding, in some degree of sympathy, also to his genuine moral indignation at the administration's lack of candor in dealing with many issues of foreign policy. One of the leading antirevisionist historians has commented on the winter of 1940–41: "Some things that were done were wholly told, some vaguely told, and a few, such as naval talks and movements, were hardly told at all. The President's utterances of this period did not provide all the explanatory knowledge that could have been wanted to follow and judge American policy in action. . . . they were not systematic statements of the situation facing the United States and the choice before it. They were emotional appeals . . . They were exertions of leadership in behalf of measures that were secretly in the making, or rather in the taking."[52] Making all allowances for hyperbole, one can still understand Beard's resentment at this lack of candor; as he expressed it privately: "To 'save England' is every principle of constitutional government and democracy and public morality to be violated?"[53] Even if evasion or secrecy was the necessary price of politics, without which the president would have been unable to maintain needed popular support or to give adequate backing to the Allies for the sake of national security, the resulting public confusion inevitably tarnished the liberal–democratic ideal of self-government.

Yet it remains a tragedy that Beard was not willing even to admit

51. Letter to Harry Elmer Barnes, June 17 [1940?], Barnes file.
52. Herbert Feis, *The Road to Pearl Harbor,* p. 134.
53. Letter to Oswald Garrison Villard, July 17 [no year], Villard Papers.

the possibility that history, not President Roosevelt, had made continentalism an archaic conception. Carl Becker caught Beard's personality in a phrase when he called him a "hard-headed idealist" who was both "an exasperated cynic" and "a warm-hearted friend of suffering humanity."[54] Yet in the end it was the shy, aloof "Man of Letters" who was the more hard-headed, being fully aware that "history is a cynical, tough old nut that always betrays our ideal aspirations."[55] Revolutions are not betrayed, Becker knew, only the hopes of their leaders. Future historians may well conclude that it was history, not any man, who betrayed Beard's hopes. In his last years he lost much of that confident poise and serenity which had made him, in the eyes of his friends, such an appealing blend of Indiana farmer and Roman philosopher. He had become deeply suspicious of internationalist policy-makers, touched on the raw by criticism from fellow historians, and grievously convinced that he and his cause were persecuted.[56] The postwar world appalled him. He could not see in the wreck of his hopes the building of a new world in which the common interests and ideals of America and Western Europe counted for more than their differences. "Frankly," he wrote, "as I read the astounding revelations that come out each morning, I am utterly speechless."[57] His hopes had crumbled around him, cruelly dimming the light of his own understanding. His dream of the Promise of American Life must have seemed even more remote than it had been before the Depression when he saluted the new technology that would usher in "the dawn and not the dusk of the gods." "When I come to the end," he had once prophesied, "my mind will still be beating its wings against thought's

54. Review of Beard's *Cross Currents in Europe To-day*, in *Nation*, 115 (1922), 553.

55. Becker, letter to Louis Gottschalk, December 26, 1938, Becker Papers.

56. I have not been granted permission to cite evidence I have seen which, in my opinion, justifies this judgment, so it must await some future day for verification or refutation by others.

57. Letter to O. G. Villard, February 9, 1946, Villard Papers.

prison."[58] On September 1, 1948, the philosopher–historian faced death. All over the world the dusk of the gods had darkly fallen, throwing into deep shadows the American Republic whose history he had so long and lovingly struggled to comprehend with such prodigal expense of energy and passion.

58. Quoted by Eric F. Goldman in his "Charles A. Beard: An Impression," in *Charles A. Beard: An Appraisal*, p. 7.

CHAPTER EIGHT

Point of Departure

A GREAT MAN, as Justice Holmes pointed out, represents "a strategic point in the campaign of history, and part of his greatness consists in his being *there*."[1] Carl Becker and Charles Beard earned a distinguished place in American thought by their leadership in the revolt against the dogmas of scientific history. It was part of their greatness that they recognized the need in America to rethink the philosophy of history in the light of modern tendencies of thought, as philosophers and historians in Europe had for some time been doing. Whether or not Becker and Beard were successful in establishing a new basis for historical knowledge, they served their cause with courage and style. From an abstract point of view it is easy to emphasize their limitations. As philosophers they posed more problems than they could solve, and their ideas seem fragmentary and unsystematic by comparison with those of the great thinkers. Even as historians they had marked shortcomings. Becker was at his best within the narrow limits of the interpretive essay, and his mind hovered closely over a few ideas and a small territory of history. Beard's range was astonishing, encompassing the whole career of American civilization, yet his reach inevitably exceeded his grasp, the rigidity of his economic interpretation compelling later revision of many of his conclusions. But, in a more concrete perspective, to point to their limitations is only to define their

1. "John Marshall," *The Mind and Faith of Justice Holmes*, ed. Max Lerner (Boston, 1943), p. 383.

talents. They explored for their generation the implications for history of vital modern ideas, and their historical writings brought fresh understanding and vivid synthesis to the American past. As thoughtful liberals living in an age of upheaval, they expounded and illuminated the great public issues of the day.

Above all, Becker and Beard did much to humanize the study of history in America. If they were skeptics, skepticism was needed to challenge the myths of scientific history. They taught historians professional sophistication, undermining the naïve confidence which had supported both the arrogance of speculative theories of the fixed course of historical development and the aridity of dull chronicles of disparate data. This historical positivism had tended to dehumanize the historian and his subject. Becker's studies in climates of opinion and representative men and Beard's analysis of civilization in terms of the ideas and interests of planters, farmers, workers, and capitalists shared a healthy impulse to bring concrete life to the narration of American history.

Although this revolt against pseudoscience, finality, and formalism was fundamentally creative, it did not fully accomplish its aims. It was dogged by the tradition it attacked and distorted by an exaggerated pragmatism. If one is to shoot at a king, one must be sure to kill him. With Becker and Beard historical skepticism was partly due to a failure to overthrow the despotism of positivistic ideas. Skepticism need not result from the recognition that the event on the historian's page is not the actual event or any copy of it. The historian can only construct an ideal event from the traces of actual events reflected in and reported on by documents. But this ideal construction represents the answers to his questions; it is not, any more than physics is for the scientist, a poor substitute for reality. If the past could be dredged up by collective total recall or magically reproduced in fact, the historian would still have to construct an ideal event in order to tell a significant story. The authority of historical knowledge requires only the possibility of an intellectually responsible, or verifiable, inquiry. The value of historical knowledge depends upon the power of the historian to comprehend a sequence of human development as an intelligible pattern. Becker and Beard could not support this authority and this power because they were still haunted by the abstract ideal of true explanation as the total reproduction of the past or the fixing of historical events according to laws. The shadow of historical positivism threw their skepticism into relief, and it was intensified by their pragmatic view of thought as an instrument of practical adjustment. Exaggerating the importance of the historian's hopes and fears, they tended to reduce the historical imagination to a mere weapon in present struggles.

Yet the involvement of the historian in actual history, though it generates his interest in certain problems, need not, any more than the scientist's involvement in nature, stifle his objectivity in assessing the evidence according to the highest critical standards of his profession. If the relative stability, the impersonality, and the universality of these standards in the field of natural science make the scientist's pursuit of disinterestedness much easier than the historian's, the historian has the advantage of not seeking or needing the kind of mathematical precision appropriate to physics. Modern man has transformed nature into something rich and strange, making ever more fallacious and pathetic the pathetic fallacy. The scientist's nature is not the dappled splendor which the poet celebrates but the impersonal system that follows from the mathematical elaboration of precise readings of instruments. Yet when nature had been thus reduced to a system of general causes, it became increasingly clear that historical life was recalcitrant to scientific treatment, and the way was open for recognizing a new approach to a different kind of reality. The more nature was scientifically *explained*, the less it could be *understood* in human terms of purpose and value, just as, so long as it was *understood* in this sense, it could not be *explained*. In this paradox the essential difference between history and nature is revealed, for the understanding of history was inhibited whenever the effort was made to explain it scientifically in terms of abstract causal relationships. Man can only try to understand his own doings, seeing in them the intelligibility that is the objectification of his own intelligence, purpose, and will. "The Sphinx," as Emerson said, "must solve her own riddle."[2]

Becker and Beard were groping for some basic distinction between science and history, but the cleavage they stressed tended to be invidious, at the expense of history, making its unscientific character equivalent to its frailty as a mode of knowledge. In the effort to prevent the naïve assimilation of history by science they overdramatized the differences, and in doing so they promoted a misunderstanding of both disciplines. The historian, they said, could not explain the past as a fixed course of events determined inexorably by a universal system of overarching laws, compelling all things to their sway; but Becker and Beard were not sufficiently aware that this dream of science, which seemed to them to be a nightmare, has been discarded by scientists themselves. In the light of 20th-century physics the attempts made by 19th-century historical positivists to create a science of history were based on obsolete conceptions of science. Einstein's theory of relativity has pointed up the inescapability in science of spatial and temporal frames of reference, and Heisenberg's principle of indeterminacy, based on the scientific observer's inability to determine accurately both the position and the velocity of an electron at the same time, has supplanted the confidence in absolute and universal predictive certainty with the modest recognition of statistical probability and a margin of intrinsic uncertainty. In the perspective of modern science both the scientist and the historian share to some extent a common situation. Both investigators are necessarily affected by the worlds they explore; minds without contact with nature or history could not interpret either instruments or documents; and both documents and instruments participate in and modify the structure they are intended to reveal. Discoveries in both history and science react upon

2. "History," in Essays, First Series, Standard Library Edition, 2, 10. See José Ortega y Gasset, Concord and Liberty (New York, Norton, 1946), p. 145.

and transform critical standards and procedures, as well as the practical conduct of life, just because both disciplines, since they rest upon critical thought instead of dogma, must ever be open to the revision of further thought and experience.[3] It is true that the historian's subjectivity is peculiar to his work in the sense that he must employ his experience, feelings, and imaginative sympathy in order to revivify the life expressed in the symbols he studies, whereas the scientist rigorously strives for impersonality in his language and implements. Yet modern scientists have emphasized the idea that knowledge of nature cannot be divorced from the character of the instruments used to obtain it. "In science," A. S. Eddington has said, "we study the linkage of pointer readings with pointer readings," and the scientific mind seems ultimately to find itself in its object, "regaining from Nature that which the mind has put into Nature."[4]

In their recoil against the fallacies of 19th-century historical positivism Becker and Beard woke historians from their dogmatic slumbers at the price of a skepticism which, instead of being constructively provisional, threatened to become destructively final. From the specter of chaos which they had invoked they sought refuge in a theory of progress which made sense out of history only by organizing it through its relation to an arbitrary and vague goal. In this way utopia becomes the debtors' prison of historians who declare history bankrupt. By an ironic twist of the dialectic of the antiformalist revolt, with its faith in the scientific control of the historical process, Becker and Beard succumbed to an ideological formalism at odds with both the historical spirit and the liberal mind. The liberal necessarily must stand for the critical revision of

3. For these common elements in history and science see Edgar Wind, "Some Points of Contact between History and Natural Science," in *Philosophy and History: Essays Presented to Ernst Cassirer,* ed. Raymond Klibansky and H. J. Paton (Oxford, Oxford University Press, 1936), pp. 255–64.

4. *The Nature of the Physical World* (New York, Macmillan, 1929), pp. 244, 260.

traditional forms in the light of historical change, but he needs to be on guard against a technocratic rationalism which substitutes for concrete historical awareness a rigid ideology, dreams of planning history as one might build an engine, and expects from technology the realization of hopes no machine can validate. The historical process, for the liberal mind, can have no terminus or ideal fulfillment except in the perpetual and arduous work of dealing with the conflicts of the present in a temper sophisticated by a historically disciplined intelligence. To earn one's past by understanding it is the essential preparation for a future which will not be a dead end. Freedom and justice in free societies are not the bread and circuses of some far-off "good society"; they are, instead, the current consequences of reverence for the moral, political, and legal procedures of liberal democracy. This much formalism, which gives to the liberal means of political action the cherished status of ends, is necessary if antiformalism is not to nourish anarchy or despotism.

Like the liberal spirit itself, historical thought must grow and thrive upon criticism. Provocative and creative even in its failures, the thinking of Carl Becker and Charles Beard stimulates that necessary renewal. Making no pretense to finality, they prepared the way for others who now inherit their problems. Intellectual pioneers who propose new problems seldom solve them; that is the work of the future. It will certainly demand the kind of intellectual courage which these two historians possessed in such humbling abundance.

Bibliography

A full listing of works consulted would be much too ponderous for a book of this size. I have recorded below only those cited or mentioned in my text or notes. For the convenience of the reader I have arranged the entries according to their primary place in a framework of categories which reflects my particular exploitation of the materials. The Becker Papers are in the Mann Library at Cornell University; the Villard Papers in the Houghton Library at Harvard University; the Barnes File in the possession of Harry Elmer Barnes.

BIOGRAPHICAL

Beard, Mary R., *The Making of Charles A. Beard,* New York, Exposition Press, 1955.

"Charles A. Beard," *Current Biography* (1941), 51–4.

Counts, George, "Charles Beard, the Public Man," *Charles A. Beard: An Appraisal,* ed. Howard K. Beale (Lexington, University of Kentucky Press, 1954), pp. 231–53.

Curti, Merle E., "A Great Teacher's Teacher," *Social Education, 13* (1949), 263–6, 274.

Goldman, Eric F., "Charles A. Beard: An Impression," *Charles A. Beard: An Appraisal,* ed. Howard K. Beale (Lexington, University of Kentucky Press, 1954), pp. 1–7.

Josephson, Matthew, "Charles A. Beard: A Memoir," *Virginia Quarterly Review, 25* (1949), 585–602.

Macmahon, Arthur W., "Charles Austin Beard as a Teacher," *Political Science Quarterly, 65* (1950), 1–19.

Phillips, Harlan B., "Charles Beard, Walter Vrooman, and the Founding of Ruskin Hall," *South Atlantic Quarterly, 50* (1951), 186–91.

Sabine, George H., "Carl Lotus Becker," intro. to Becker, *Freedom and Responsibility in the American Way of Life* (New York, Knopf, 1945) pp. vii–xlii.

Smith, Charlotte Watkins, *Carl Becker: On History and the Climate of Opinion*, Ithaca, Cornell University Press, 1956.

BY CHARLES A. BEARD

"Ruskin and the Babble of Tongues," *New Republic, 87* (1936), 370–2.

BY CARL L. BECKER

"On Being a Professor," *Unpopular Review, 7* (1917), 342–61.

THE TRADITION OF SCIENTIFIC HISTORY

Adams, George B., "History and the Philosophy of History," *American Historical Review, 14* (1909), 221–36.
Adams, Henry, *The Degradation of the Democratic Dogma*, intro. by Brooks Adams, New York, Macmillan, 1920.
———— *The Education of Henry Adams*, New York, Modern Library, 1931.
———— *Henry Adams and His Friends: A Collection of His Unpublished Letters*, comp. Harold Dean Cater, Boston, Houghton Mifflin, 1947.
Adams, Herbert Baxter, "Seminary Libraries and University Extension," *Johns Hopkins University Studies in History and Political Science, 5* (1887), 437–69.
American Historical Association, "The Meeting of the A.H.A. at Chicago," *American Historical Review, 10* (1905), 489–508.
———— "Proceedings," *Annual Report, 1* (1901), 19–38.
Bennett, Charles W., "The Ranke Library in America," in American Historical Association, *Papers, 3* (1889), 131–3.
Bourne, Edward Gaylord, *Essays in Historical Criticism*, New York, Scribner's, 1901.
Cassirer, Ernst, *The Problem of Knowledge*, trans. W. H. Woglom and C. W. Hendel, New Haven, Yale University Press, 1950.
Channing, Edward, "Justin Winsor," *American Historical Review, 3* (1898), 197–202.
Cheyney, Edward, "Law in History," *American Historical Review, 29* (1924), 231–48.
Ely, Richard T., "A Sketch of the Life and Services of Herbert Baxter Adams," *Herbert Baxter Adams: Tributes of Friends* (Baltimore, Johns Hopkins University Press, 1902), pp. 27–49.

Emerson, Donald E., "Hildrith, Draper, and Scientific History," *Historiography and Urbanization: Essays in American History in Honor of W. Stull Holt*, ed., Eric F. Goldman (Baltimore, Johns Hopkins University Press, 1941), pp. 139–70.

Fling, Fred Morrow, *The Writing of History: An Introduction to Historical Method*, New Haven, Yale University Press, 1920.

Holt, W. Stull, "The Idea of Scientific History in America," *Journal of the History of Ideas*, 1 (1940), 352–62.

Jordy, William, *Henry Adams: Scientific Historian*, New Haven, Yale University Press, 1952.

Kraus, Michael, *A History of American History*, New York, Farrar and Rinehart, 1937.

Osgood, Herbert A., "Study of American Colonial History," in American Historical Association, *Annual Report* (1898), 61–76.

Smith, Theodore Clarke, "The Writing of American History in America, from 1884 to 1934," *American Historical Review*, 40 (1935), 439–49.

Strout, Cushing, "Historical Thought in America," *Virginia Quarterly Review*, 28 (1952), 242–57.

Welling, James C., *Connecticut Federalism*, New York, New York Historical Society, 1890.

White, Andrew D., *Autobiography* (London, Macmillan, 1905), Vol. 1.

——— "On Studies in General History and the History of Civilization," in American Historical Association, *Papers*, 1 (1886), 49–72.

THE REVOLT AGAINST SCIENTIFIC HISTORY

Arendt, Hannah, "Understanding and Politics," *Partisan Review*, 20 (1953), 377–92.

Barnes, Harry Elmer, "James Harvey Robinson," *American Masters of Social Science*, ed. Howard Odum (New York, Holt, 1927), pp. 321–408.

——— *The New History and the Social Studies*, New York, 1925.

Cohen, Morris R., *The Meaning of Human History*, LaSalle, Ill., Open Court, 1947.

Collingwood, R. G., *The Idea of History*, Oxford, Oxford University Press, 1946.

Croce, Benedetto, *History as the Story of Liberty*, trans. Sylvia Sprigge, New York, Norton, 1941.

Destler, Chester McArthur, "Some Observations on Contemporary Historical Theory," *American Historical Review,* 55 (1950), 503–29.

Dewey, John, *Logic: The Theory of Inquiry,* New York, Holt, 1938.

—— *The Philosophy of John Dewey,* ed. Joseph Ratner, New York, Holt, 1928.

Eddington, A. S., *The Nature of the Physical World,* New York, Macmillan, 1929.

Frankel, Charles, *The Case for Modern Man,* New York, Harper, 1955.

James, William, *A Pluralistic Universe,* ed., Ralph Barton Perry, New York, Longmans, Green, 1943.

—— *The Principles of Psychology* (London, Macmillan, 1891), Vol. 1.

Malin, James C., *On the Nature of History: Essays about History and Dissidence,* Ann Arbor, Mich., 1954.

Mandelbaum, Maurice, *The Problem of Historical Knowledge,* New York, Liveright, 1938.

Mannheim, Karl, *Ideology and Utopia: An Introduction to the Sociology of Knowledge,* trans. Louis Wirth and Edward Shils, New York, Harcourt, Brace, 1949.

Morison, Samuel Eliot, "Faith of a Historian," *American Historical Review,* 56 (1951), 261–75.

Oakeshott, Michael, *Experience and Its Modes,* Cambridge, Cambridge University Press, 1933.

Ortega y Gasset, José, *Concord and Liberty,* trans. Helene Weyl, New York, Norton, 1946.

Popper, Karl R., *The Open Society and Its Enemies,* rev. ed. Princeton, Princeton University Press, 1950.

Read, Conyers, "The Social Responsibilities of the Historian," *American Historical Review,* 55 (1950), 275–85.

Robinson, James Harvey, *The Mind in the Making: The Relation of Intelligence to Social Reform,* New York, Harper, 1921.

—— *The New History: Essays Illustrating the Modern Historical Outlook,* New York, Harper, 1922.

—— "The Newer Ways of Historians," *American Historical Review,* 35 (1930), 245–55.

Sorenson, Lloyd R., "Charles A. Beard and German Historical Thought," *Mississippi Valley Historical Review,* 42 (1955), 274–87.

Turner, Frederick Jackson, *The Early Writings of Frederick Jackson Turner,* intro. by Fulmer Mood, Madison, University of Wisconsin Press, 1938.
—— *The Frontier in American History,* New York, Holt, 1921.
Wind, Edgar, "Some Points of Contact between History and Natural Science," *Philosophy and History: Essays Presented to Ernst Cassirer,* ed. Raymond Klibansky and H. J. Paton (Oxford, Oxford University Press, 1936), pp. 255–64.

BY CHARLES A. BEARD

"Books That Changed Our Minds," *New Republic,* 97 (1938), 206. Contribution to a symposium.
A Charter for the Social Sciences in the Schools, American Historical Association, Report of the Commission on the Social Studies, Pt. I, New York, Scribner's, 1932.
The Discussion of Human Affairs, New York, Macmillan, 1936.
"Grounds for a Reconsideration of Historiography," *Theory and Practice in Historical Study: A Report of the Committee on Historiography,* ed. Merle E. Curti, Social Science Research Council, *Bulletin,* 54 (1946), 1–14.
"Henry Adams," *New Republic,* 22 (1920), 162–3.
"History and History," *Nation,* 111 (1920), 416–17.
"History and Social Science," *Saturday Review of Literature,* 12 (1935), 9, 22–3.
"James Ford Rhodes," *New Republic,* 21 (1919), 82–3.
The Nature of the Social Sciences, in Relation to Objectives of Instruction, American Historical Association, Report of the Commission on the Social Studies, Pt. VII, New York, Scribner's, 1934.
"Problems of Terminology in Historical Writing: The Need for Greater Precision in the Use of Historical Terms," *Theory and Practice in Historical Study: A Report of the Committee on Historiography,* ed. Merle E. Curti, Social Science Research Council, *Bulletin,* 54 (1946), 103–8.
Review of Carl L. Becker, *The Heavenly City of the Eighteenth-century Philosophers,* in *American Historical Review,* 38 (1933), 590–1.
Review of R. G. Collingwood, *The Idea of History,* in *American Historical Review,* 52 (1947), 704–7.
"That Noble Dream," *American Historical Review,* 41 (1935), 74–87.

"Written History As an Act of Faith," *American Historical Review, 39* (1934), 219–29.

(with Alfred Vagts) "Currents of Thought in Historiography," *American Historical Review, 42* (1937), 460–83.

BY CARL L. BECKER

"Books That Changed Our Minds," *New Republic, 97* (1938), 135. Contribution to a symposium.

"A Chronicle of Facts," *New Republic, 25* (1921), 382–3.

"Detachment and the Writing of History," *Atlantic, 106* (1910), 524–36.

Everyman His Own Historian: Essays on History and Politics, New York, Appleton Century Crofts, 1935. See esp. "The Education of Henry Adams," "Henry Adams Once More," "Labelling the Historians," "Everyman His Own Historian," and "Mr. Wells and the New History."

"The Function of the Social Sciences," *Science and Man,* ed. Ruth Nanda Anshen (New York, Harcourt Brace, 1942), pp. 243–69.

"German Historians and the Great War," *Dial, 60* (1916), 160–4.

"History as the Intellectual Adventure of Mankind," *New Republic, 30* (1922), 174–6.

"James Harvey Robinson," *Nation, 144* (1937), 48–50.

"Learning and the Life of Man," *Return to Freedom,* ed. Thomas H. Johnson (New York, Putnam's, 1944), pp. 5–22.

"Miscellaneous," Notes, Drawer 15, Becker Papers. On William James, on Relativity, and on E. A. Robinson's "Modernites."

"The New History," *Dial, 53* (1912), 19–22.

"A New Philosophy of History," *Dial, 59* (1915), 146–8.

"On Historical Evidence," MS, Becker Papers.

Review of A. N. Whitehead's *Adventures in Ideas,* in *American Historical Review, 39* (1933), 87–9.

Review of F. J. Teggart, *The Processes of History,* in *American Historical Review, 24* (1919), 266–8.

Review of Henry Adams, *The Degradation of the Democratic Dogma,* in *American Historical Review, 25* (1920), 480–2.

Review of Henry O. Taylor, *A Historian's Creed,* Gaetano Salvemini, *Historian and Scientist,* and Sir Charles Oman, *On the Writing of History,* in *American Historical Review, 45* (1940), 591–3.

Review of Maurice Mandelbaum, *The Problem of Historical Knowledge,* in *Philosophical Review, 49* (1940), 361–4.

"The Reviewing of Historical Books," American Historical Association, *Annual Report* (1912), 127–36.

"Some Aspects of the Influence of Social Problems and Ideas upon the Studying and Writing of History," *Publications of the American Sociological Society, 7* (1913), 73–112.

"The Subjective Object and Vice Versa," *New Republic, 85* (1936), 256.

"What Is Historiography?" *American Historical Review, 44* (1938), 20–8.

"What Are Historical Facts?" *Western Political Quarterly, 8* (1955), 327–40.

LETTERS

From: W. Stull Holt, January 13, 1932, Becker Papers. *To:* Conyers Read, December 3, 1944, Becker Papers; Frederick Jackson Turner (draft), May 15, 1910, Becker Papers.

THE REVOLT AGAINST FORMALISM

Blinkoff, Maurice, *The Influence of Charles A. Beard upon American Historiography,* University of Buffalo Studies, *12,* Monographs in History, 4 (1936).

Brown, Robert E., *Charles Beard and the Constitution: A Critical Analysis of "An Economic Interpretation of the Constitution,"* Princeton, Princeton University Press, 1956.

Cowley, Malcolm and Bernard Smith, *Books That Changed Our Minds,* New York, Kelmscott, 1939.

Goldman, Eric F., *Rendezvous with Destiny: A History of Modern American Reform,* New York, Knopf, 1952.

Higham, John A., "The Rise of American Intellectual History," *American Historical Review, 56* (1951), 453–71.

Hirschfeld, Charles, "Edward Eggleston: Pioneer in Social History," *Historiography and Urbanization: Essays in Honor of W. Stull Holt,* ed. Eric F. Goldman (Baltimore, Johns Hopkins University Press, 1941), pp. 189–210.

Hofstadter, Richard, "Beard and the Constitution," *American Quarterly, 2* (1950), 195–213.

Holmes, O. W., Jr., Letter to Sir Frederick Pollock, June 20, 1928, in *The*

Mind and Faith of Justice Holmes, ed. Max Lerner, Boston, Little Brown, 1943.

Lerner, Max, "Beard's 'Economic Interpretation,' " No. 9 of "Books That Changed Our Minds," *New Republic, 99* (1939), 7–11.

Seligman, E. R. A., *The Economic Interpretation of History,* New York, Columbia University Press, 1902.

Simons, Algie M., *Social Forces in American History,* New York, Macmillan, 1911.

Thomas, Robert E., "A Reappraisal of Charles A. Beard's *An Economic Interpretation of the Constitution of the United States,*" *American Historical Review, 57* (1952), 370–5.

White, Morton G., *Social Thought in America: The Revolt Against Formalism,* New York, Viking, 1949.

BY CHARLES A. BEARD

American Government and Politics, New York, Macmillan, 1910.

The American Party Battle, New York, Macmillan, 1928.

Contemporary American History, 1877–1913, New York, Macmillan, 1914.

"Co-operation and the New Century," *Young Oxford, 2* (1900), 96–100.

The Economic Basis of Politics, 3d ed., rev., New York, Knopf, 1945.

"The Economic Basis of Politics," *New Republic, 32* (1922), 128–9.

An Economic Interpretation of the Constitution of the United States, New York, Macmillan, 1913.

Economic Origins of Jeffersonian Democracy, New York, Macmillan, 1915.

"Fresh Air in American Letters," *Nation, 124* (1927), 561–2.

"The Frontier in American History," *New Republic, 97* (1939), 359–62.

"Historiography and the Constitution," *The Constitution Reconsidered,* ed. Conyers Read (New York, Columbia University Press, 1938), pp. 159–66.

The Industrial Revolution, preface by F. York Powell, London, Sonnenschein, 1901.

"Internationalism in the United States," *New Review, 3* (1915), 159–60.

Introduction to the 1935 ed. of *An Economic Interpretation of the Constitution of the United States,* New York, Macmillan, 1939.

An Introduction to the English Historians, New York, Macmillan, 1906.

The Office of Justice of the Peace in England, in Its Origin and Development, New York, Columbia University Press, 1904.

"Political Science," *Research in the Social Sciences: Its Fundamental Methods and Objectives,* ed. Wilson Gee, New York, Macmillan, 1929, 269–91.

The Republic: Conversations on Fundamentals, New York, Viking, 1943.

The Supreme Court and the Constitution, New York, Macmillan, 1926.

The Unique Function of Education in American Democracy, Educational Policies Commission, Washington, National Education Association, 1937.

ed., *Whither Mankind: A Panorama of Modern Civilization,* New York, Longman's, Green, 1928.

"Why Study Socialism?" *The Intercollegiate Socialist,* 1 (1913), 3.

(with Mary R. Beard) *America in Midpassage,* 2 vols. New York, Macmillan, 1939.

—— *American Citizenship,* New York, Macmillan, 1914.

—— *A Basic History of the United States,* New York, Doubleday Doran, 1944.

—— *The Making of American Civilization,* New York, Macmillan, 1937.

—— *The Rise of American Civilization,* rev. college ed., 2 vols. in 1, New York, Macmillan, 1934.

(with James Harvey Robinson) *The Development of Modern Europe: An Introduction to the Study of Current History,* 2 vols. New York, Ginn, 1907–8.

LETTERS

To: Carl L. Becker, September 26 [no year]; February 4 [no year], Becker Papers.

BY CARL L. BECKER

Beginnings of the American People, The Riverside History of the United States, ed. William E. Dodd (Boston, Houghton Mifflin, 1915), Vol. 1.

"Benjamin Franklin," *Dictionary of American Biography,* 6 (1943), 585–98.

Cornell University: Founders and the Founding, Ithaca, Cornell University Press, 1943.

The Declaration of Independence: A Study in the History of Political Ideas, intro. by C. L. Becker, New York, Knopf, 1942.

The Eve of the Revolution, The Chronicles of America Series, ed. Allen Johnson (New Haven, Yale University Press, 1918), Vol. 2.

Everyman His Own Historian: Essays on History and Politics, New York, Appleton Century Crofts, 1935. See esp. "Kansas," "John Jay and Peter

Van Schaack," "The Spirit of '76," "Frederick Jackson Turner," "The
Memoirs and the Letters of Madame Roland."

"Fresh Air in American History," *Nation, 129* (1927), 559–60.

"Harnessing History," *New Republic, 22* (1920), 322.

The Heavenly City of the Eighteenth-century Philosophers, New Haven, Yale
University Press, 1932.

"The History of Political Parties in the Province of New York, 1760–
1776," *Bulletin of the University of Wisconsin,* History Series, *2* (1909),
1–320.

"Idealistic Forces in American History," *Dial, 56* (1914), 140–2.

"Memorandum Concerning a Department of Biography," MS, Becker
Papers.

Modern History, rev. ed. New York, Silver Burdett, 1941.

LETTERS

To: Charles A. Beard, May 10, 1943, Becker Papers; Louis Gottschalk,
September 3, 1944, Becker Papers.

PROGRESS AND POLITICS

Adler, Selig, "The War-Guilt Question and American Disillusionment,
1918–28," *Journal of Modern History, 23* (1951), 1–28.

Barnes, Harry Elmer, "Assessing the Blame for the World War: A Revised
Judgment Based on All the Available Documents," *Current History,
20* (1924), 171–95.

——— ed., *Perpetual War for Perpetual Peace,* Caldwell, Idaho, Caxton,
1953.

Butterfield, H., *The Whig Interpretation of History,* New York, Scribner's,
1951.

Coyle, Wayne S., *America First: The Battle Against Intervention,* Madison,
University of Wisconsin Press, 1953.

Feis, Herbert, *The Road to Pearl Harbor: The Coming of the War between the
United States and Japan,* Princeton, Princeton University Press, 1950.

——— "War Came at Pearl Harbor: Suspicions and Surmises," *Yale Review, 45* (1956), 378–90.

Ferrell, Robert H., "Pearl Harbor and the Revisionists," *Historian, 17*
(1955), 215–33.

Gershoy, Leo, "Carl Becker on Progress and Power," *American Historical Review*, 55 (1949), 22–35.

Leighton, George R., "Beard and Foreign Policy," *Charles A. Beard: An Appraisal*, ed. Howard K. Beale (Lexington, University of Kentucky Press, 1954), pp. 161–84.

Lindbergh, Brig. Gen. Charles A., Letter to Cushing Strout, September 26, 1956.

Rauch, Basil, *From Munich to Pearl Harbor: A Study in the Creation of a Foreign Policy*, New York, Creative Age, 1950.

Snyder, Phil, "Carl L. Becker and the Great War: A Crisis for a Humane Intelligence," *Western Political Quarterly*, 9 (1956), 1–10.

Strout, Cushing, "The Twentieth-Century Enlightenment," *American Political Science Review*, 49 (1955), 321–39.

"The Tangled Web" editorial in the Chicago *Daily Tribune* (April 5, 1948), p. 18.

BY CHARLES A. BEARD

The Administration and Politics of Tokyo: A Survey and Opinions, New York, Macmillan, 1923.

"America's 'Duty' to England," *Events*, 2 (1937), 327–31.

American Foreign Policy in the Making, 1932–1940: A Study in Responsibilities, New Haven, Yale University Press, 1946.

"A Call upon Every Citizen," *Harper's*, 137 (1918), 655–6.

"Collective Security: A Debate; Reply to Mr. Browder," *New Republic*, 93 (1938), 356–9.

"A Communication: Perils of Diplomacy," *New Republic*, 11 (1917), 136–8.

Cross Currents in Europe To-day, Boston, Marshall Jones, 1922.

The Devil Theory of War, New York, Vanguard, 1936.

"Emerging Issues in America," *Current History*, 41 (1934), 203–9.

"A 'Five-Year Plan' for America," *Forum*, 86 (1931), 1–11.

A Foreign Policy for America, New York, Knopf, 1940.

Giddy Minds and Foreign Quarrels: An Estimate of American Foreign Policy, New York, Macmillan, 1939.

" 'Going Ahead' with Roosevelt," *Events*, 1 (1937), 9–12.

"The Great American Tradition," *Nation*, 123 (1926), 7–8.

"Heroes and Villains of the World War," *Current History*, 24 (1926), 730–5.

"A Historian's Quest for Light," *Proceedings of the Association of History Teachers of the Middle States and Maryland, 29* (1931), 12–21.

Introduction to J. B. Bury, *The Idea of Progress: An Inquiry into Its Growth and Origin* (New York, Macmillan, 1932), pp. ix–xl.

Letter of Resignation from Columbia University, *School and Society, 6* (1917), 446–7.

"Looking Backward," *New Republic, 101* (1939), 74–80.

"National Politics and War," *Scribner's, 97* (1935), 65–70.

"On Keeping Out of War," *Current History, 43* (1936), 625–32.

"Our Choice in Foreign Policy," *Events, 1* (1937), 161–5.

President Roosevelt and the Coming of the War, 1941; A Study in Appearance and Realities, New Haven, Yale University Press, 1948.

"Prospects for Peace," *Harper's, 158* (1929), 320–30.

"Roosevelt's Place in History," *Events, 3* (1938), 81–6.

"A Search for the Center: A Challenge to Competent Minds," *Scribner's, 91* (1932), 2–7.

"A Statement by Charles A. Beard," *New Republic, 13* (1917), 249–51.

"The Study and Teaching of Politics," *Columbia University Quarterly, 12* (1910), 268–74.

Testimony before Senate Foreign Relations Committee, *Congressional Record,* 77th Congress, 1st session, 87:10 (February 13, 1941), pp. A625–7; before House Committee on Naval Affairs, "Statement of Dr. Charles A. Beard, Historian," February 10, 1938, *House Committee on Naval Affairs, Hearings on House Resolution 9218,* 75th Congress, 3d session, pp. 2133–46.

"That Promise of American Life," *New Republic, 81* (1935), 350–2.

"Those Old-World Quarrels," *Events, 2* (1937), 257–62.

"Time, Technology, and the Creative Spirit in Political Science," *American Political Science Review, 21* (1927), 1–11.

ed., *Toward Civilization,* New York, Longmans, Green, 1930.

"Whom Does Congress Represent?" *Harper's, 160* (1930), 144–52.

"Why Did We Go to War?" *New Republic, 90* (1937), 127–9.

"The World as I Want It," *Forum, 91* (1934), 332–4.

(with Mary R. Beard) *The American Spirit: A Study of the Idea of Civilization in the United States,* New York, Macmillan, 1942.

(with William Beard) *The American Leviathan: The Republic in the Machine Age,* New York, Macmillan, 1930.

(with Frederick A. Ogg) *National Governments and the World War*, New York, Macmillan, 1919.

(with George Radin) *The Balkan Pivot: Yugoslavia, a Study in Government and Administration*, New York, Macmillan, 1929.

(with George H. E. Smith) *The Idea of National Interest: An Analytical Study in American Foreign Policy*, New York, Macmillan, 1934.

—— *The Open Door at Home: A Trial Philosophy of National Interest*, New York, Macmillan, 1935.

LETTERS

To: Harry Elmer Barnes, August 7 [no year]; June 17 [1940?]; Barnes File; Oswald Garrison Villard, July 17 [no year]; July 18 [1945?]; February 9, 1946; Villard Papers.

BY CARL L. BECKER

America's War Aims and Peace Plans, War Information Series, 21, Washington, Committee on Public Information, 1918.

"Assessing the Blame for the World War: A Symposium," *Current History*, *20* (1924), 455–6.

Everyman His Own Historian: Essays on History and Politics, New York, Appleton Century Crofts, 1935. See esp. "The Modern Leviathan," "The Marxian Philosophy of History," "Freedom of Speech," "Liberalism—A Way Station," "The Dilemma of Diderot."

"A Fine Pair of Words," *Yale Review*, *23* (1934), 814–17.

"German Attempts to Divide Belgium," *A League of Nations*, *1* (1918), 307–42.

Freedom and Responsibility in the American Way of Life, intro by George H. Sabine, New York, Knopf, 1945.

"How to Keep Out of War," *Nation*, *146* (1938), 378. Contribution to a symposium.

How New Will the Better World Be? A Discussion of Post-War Reconstruction, New York, Knopf, 1944.

"The King of Beasts," MS, Becker Papers.

Modern Democracy, New Haven, Yale University Press, 1941.

"The Monroe Doctrine and the War," *Minnesota History Bulletin*, *2* (1917), 61–8.

"Mr. Wilson at the Peace Conference," *Nation*, *116* (1923), 186–8.

New Liberties for Old, New Haven, Yale University Press, 1941.
Progress and Power, Stanford, Stanford University Press, 1936.
Review of Charles A. Beard, *Cross Currents in Europe To-Day,* in *Nation,*
115 (1922), 552–3.
"Tender and Tough-Minded Historians," *Dial, 65* (1918), 106–9.
The United States: An Experiment in Democracy, New York, Harper, 1920.
"What We Didn't Know Hurt Us a Lot," *Yale Review, 32* (1944), 385–404.
"Why Europe Fights," *Cornell Alumni News, 42* (1939), 33. Contribution
to a symposium.

LETTERS

To: Richard A. Newhall, March 24, 1920, Becker Papers; William E.
Dodd, June 17, 1920; February 26, 1923; November 29, 1932; Becker
Papers; Harry Elmer Barnes, February 21, 1926, Becker Papers; Freder-
ick Lewis Allen, March 19, 1933, Becker Papers; Editor of Washington
Herald, November 26, 1935, Becker Papers; Louis Gottschalk, Decem-
ber 26, 1938, Becker Papers; Charles A. Beard [no date; probably
February, 1939], Becker Papers.

MISCELLANEOUS

Congressional References to Beard, *Congressional Record,* 77th Congress,
1st session, 87:2 (February 22, 1941), p. 1273; 76th Congress, 2d session,
85:1 (October 31, 1939), p. 1140.
Darwin, Charles, *The Descent of Man* (New York, Appleton, 1871), Vol. 1.
Emerson, Ralph Waldo, "History," *Essays: First Series,* Standard Library
Ed. (Boston, Houghton Mifflin, 1883), pp. 9–43.
"The Poet," *Essays: Second Series,* ibid., pp. 9–45.
Hawthorne, Nathaniel, *The English Notebooks,* ed. Randall Stewart, New
York, Modern Language Association, 1941.
Home Building and Loan Association v. Blaisdell, 290 U.S. 1933.

Index

Adams, Brooks, 16, 66
Adams, George Burton, 19–20, 23, 33
Adams, Henry: theory of, 15–16; seminar of, 18; Becker's view of, 30, 132; Beard's view of, 54–5, 57 n., 58, 103; context of his work, 67; compared to Beard, 106; compared to Becker, 126
Adams, Herbert Baxter, 17–19, 22–3
Adams, Sam, 69, 72–3, 80
America First Committee, 135, 136 and n.
Antiformalism: defined, 9; Turner's plea for, 22–3, 65; growth of, 65–7; Becker's contribution to, 68; Beard's economic determinism related to, 86, 90–1, 100; and Beard's idea of progress, 108; impact on Becker's and Beard's liberalism, 115–116, 161, on Becker's, 122; limits of, 162
Aron, Raymond, 14

Bacon, Francis, 35
Barnes, Harry Elmer, 23–6, 70, 90, 115, 138, 149; Becker's view of, 25–6, 121; Beard's view of, 139
Beard, Charles A.: temperament and life compared to Becker, 4–5, 136, 155; praises Becker, 85; view of Turner, 25; relation to Robinson and Barnes, 26; relation to pragmatism, 27–8; family background and student days, 88–90; place in American thought, 157–8.
   THEORY OF KNOWLEDGE: origins of his relativism, 51; defends interpretation, 51–2, criticizes scientific

history, 52–3; on frames of reference, 53–4; on the impasse of relativism, 54; on act of faith in progress, 54–5; compared to Croce and Mannheim, 56–7; sympathy for Henry Adams, 57 n.; problem of his "act of faith," 58; basis of his skepticism, 59; relativism and explanation, 59–61.
   ANTIFORMALISM: antiformalist purpose, 86; influence of, 86–7; atmosphere at Columbia and the New School, 90; seed-bed of his economic approach, 90–2; nonpartisan spirit, 92–3, ambiguity about framers, 93–9; pragmatic approach, 100; subtlety of interpretation, 100–2; mechanical dialectic, 102–3; oversimplification, 103–4; revision of economic theory, 105–6; "realistic dialectics," 106; vision of progress, 106–8; Manichaean approach, 109–10; self-criticism, 110–11.
   PROGRESS AND POLITICS: workers' education movement, 88–9; reformer's zeal, 89–90; controversy over, 135; and "America First," 136 and n.; supports Wilson, 137; leaves Columbia, 137; and "revisionists," 138; criticism of Barnes, 139; pre-Depression confidence, 139; sources of his isolationism, 140; faith in national planning, 140–2; influenced by Nye Committee, 142–3; joins "revisionists," 143; ambivalence about F.D.R., 144; predicts Pacific war, 144; de-

fends "continentalism," 145-6; on
F.D.R.'s foreign policy, 146-9; his
partisanship, 149; succumbs to
"devil theory," 150-1; utopianism,
152-5; moral indignation, 154;
bitterness, 155-6; death, 156.

WORKS

America in Midpassage, 101, 103,
146
*American Foreign Policy in the Mak-
ing, 1932-40,* 146, 151
American Government and Politics,
92, 98
The American Leviathan, 122
The American Spirit, 109-10, 146
Basic History of the United States, 99
Cross Currents in Europe To-day, 138
The Devil Theory of War, 143
The Discussion of Human Affairs,
106
The Economic Basis of Politics, 105-6
*An Economic Interpretation of the
Constitution,* 92-9
*Economic Origins of Jeffersonian
Democracy,* 99-100
"A Five-Year Plan for America,"
141
Giddy Minds and Foreign Quarrels,
145
The Industrial Revolution, 89-90
*An Introduction to the English His-
torians,* 91
*The Office of Justice of the Peace in
England,* 90
The Open Door at Home, 141-2
*President Roosevelt and the Coming
of the War, 1941,* 146-9
The Republic, 98-9
The Rise of American Civilization,
100-4, 107, 139
"Written History as an Act of
Faith," 52-5
Beard, Mary R., 105
Becker, Carl L.: temperament and

life compared to Beard, 4-5, 136,
155; praises Beard, 86; relation to
Turner, 25, 122, to Robinson and
Barnes, 25-6, to pragmatism, 26-8;
place in American thought, 157-8.

THEORY OF KNOWLEDGE: history
and science, 30-2; historical facts,
33-5; false objectivity, 35-6; historical synthesis, 37-40; "specious
present," 39-40; relativism, 40-1,
its danger, 41-2; value of his
theory, 41; dilemma of his relativism, 42-3; ambiguity regarding
positivism, 43-4; exaggerated pragmatism, 44; ambivalence regarding
progress, 45-7; on Beard's "act of
faith," 47 n.; fallacy of "Everyman" analogy, 47-8; limited validity of his relativism, 48, 83-4;
liberating effect, 49.

ANTIFORMALISM: lesson of his
work, 68; futility of positivist history, 68-9; pluralism about motives, 69-73; role of individuals and
social forces, 72-3; ideas as events,
73-4; "climate of opinion" concept, 74-7, 82; style as evidence,
78; problem of narration and synthesis, 78-9; novelistic techniques,
79-82; problem of causality, 82-3;
conflict between his theory and
practice, 83; limitations of his concepts, 84-5; praised by Beard, 85;
praises Beard, 86.

PROGRESS AND POLITICS: faith in
Declaration, 117; source of his dilemma, 117-18; war-time idealism
(*1917*), 118-19; disillusionment
and pessimism, 119-21; on Wilson
and "revisionists," 121; influence
of Turner and Beard, 122; liberals'
dilemma, 122-4; theory of progress, 124-7; on totalitarianism, 127-
8; case for intervention, 128, 152;

Emerson, Ralph Waldo, 110, 160

Fascism, 3, 54, 105–6, 115–16, 127–8
Feis, Herbert, 150
Fiske, John, 17
Franklin, Benjamin, 68 f., 80, 132, 134

Gerry, Elbridge, 96
Gershoy, Leo, 124, 132
Gibbon, Edward, 84–5
Gibbs, Josiah Willard, 16
Goering, Hermann W., 152
Gompers, Samuel, 103
Grattan, C. Hartley, 138
Grew, Joseph C., 147

Hamilton, Alexander, 99, 149;
    Beard's view of, 94, 100, 143
Hawthorne, Nathaniel, 117
Hearst, William Randolph, 102
Heisenberg, Werner, 160
Henry County *Republican*, 88
Heussi, Karl, 52, 56
History: modern sense of, 1; crisis of,
    2; philosophy of, in America, 7;
    professional growth of, 14; school
    of New, 23–6, 39, 50, 70, 72; ex-
    planation in, 47–8, 59–61, 82–3,
    158–60; conflicts of, 133; modern
    science compared with and con-
    trasted to, 159–61.
    SCIENTIFIC: defined, 8; impact of
    Darwin on, 14–18; impact of
    Comte on, 15; Henry Adams's
    theory of, 15–16; "germ theory"
    of, 17; Rankean cult of, 18–21;
    Turner's critique of, 21–3; New
    History's critique of, 23–5; as back-
    ground for Becker and Beard, 28–
    9; Becker's critique of, 30–8, 68–9,
    73–4, 78; Becker's ambiguous re-
    lation to, 43–4; Beard's critique of,
    52–4; Beard's nostalgia for, 57–61;
    formalist influence of, 65–7; com-

pared to Beard's economic inter-
pretation, 94, 106; skepticism re-
lated to, 158, 161; its obsolete view
of science, 160
Hitler, Adolf, 127, 133, 152
Hofstadter, Richard, 90–1
Holbach, 75
Holmes, Justice Oliver Wendell, 65,
    96–7, 157
Holt, W. Stull, 49
Hume, David, 74 ff., 84
Hutchinson, Thomas, 69, 72–3, 80

Intercollegiate Socialist, 93
Isolationism: Becker's critique of,
    128, 152; Beard's critique of, 136,
    139–40 and n.; Beard's, developed,
    109–10, 116, 145–6, 150, 152–5

Jackson, Andrew, 144
James, Henry, 79, 104
James, William, 14, 26–7, 39
Jay, John, 69–70, 72
Jefferson, Thomas, 69 f., 74, 99, 123,
    133 f., 144, 149; Becker's view of,
    78; Beard's view of, 100, 143
Joyce, James, 79

Kelvin, William Thomson, 16
Keynes, John Maynard, 138
Knightstown Banner, 88

Lawrence, D. H., 85
Lerner, Max, 150
Liberalism: as modern force, 1;
    modern crisis of, 2; critics of, 3;
    defined, 9–10, and F.D.R.'s policy,
    154; and historical spirit, 161–2.
    BECKER'S: early faith, 117;
    eroded, 122–4; challenged, 127;
    revived, 128–30; dilemma of, 115–
    16, 130–4.
    BEARD'S: and Wilson, 137, 142;
    planning ideal of, 140–1; and
    F.D.R., 144, 154

Date Due